When the Girls Come Out to Play

When the Girls Come Out to Play

Teenage Working-Class Girls' Leisure between the Wars

KATHARINE MILCOY

Bloomsbury Academic
An imprint of Bloomsbury Publishing Plc

B L O O M S B U R Y
LONDON · OXFORD · NEW YORK · NEW DELHI · SYDNEY

Bloomsbury Academic
An imprint of Bloomsbury Publishing Plc

50 Bedford Square	1385 Broadway
London	New York
WC1B 3DP	NY 10018
UK	USA

www.bloomsbury.com

**BLOOMSBURY and the Diana logo are trademarks of
Bloomsbury Publishing Plc**

First published 2017

British Library Cataloguing-in-Publication Data
A catalogue record for this book is available from the British Library.

ISBN: HB: 978-1-4742-7959-8
PB: 978-1-4742-7958-1
ePDF: 978-1-4742-7960-4
eBook: 978-1-4742-7961-1

Library of Congress Cataloging-in-Publication Data
Names: Milcoy, Katharine, author.
Title: When the girls come out to play: teenage working-class girls' leisure between the wars / Katharine Milcoy.
Description: London; New York: Bloomsbury Academic, 2017. | Includes bibliographical references and index.
Identifiers: LCCN 2016051167| ISBN 9781474279598 (hb) | ISBN 9781474279581 (pb)
Subjects: LCSH: Teenage girls–Great Britain–Social conditions–20th century. | Working class–Great Britain–History–20th century. | Leisure–Great Britain–History–20th century. | Great Britain–Social conditions–20th century.
Classification: LCC HQ799.G7 M465 2017 | DDC 305.235/20941–dc23 LC record available at https://lccn.loc.gov/2016051167

Cover design by Adriana Brioso
Cover image: Spectators gain a good vantage point during the Epsom Derby in Surrey, 5th June 1929 (Photo by Topical Press Agency/Getty Images)

Typeset by Deanta Global Publishing Services, Chennai, India
Printed and bound in Great Britain

To find out more about our authors and books visit www.bloomsbury.com. Here you will find extracts, author interviews, details of forthcoming events and the option to sign up for our newsletters.

For my parents

Contents

List of illustrations

Acknowledgements

First and foremost I would like to express my gratitude to the women who shared with me, in the late 1990s, memories of their teenage years. I would like to thank the staff of numerous archives and libraries who have been most helpful: the Women's Library now at the LSE, London Metropolitan Archives, Cadbury Research Library: Special Collections, University of Birmingham, Southwark Local Studies Library, and the Cambridge University Mission for giving me access to their archives. The London Library has been an invaluable source to draw upon in terms of the breadth of its collection. Luci Gosling at the Mary Evans Picture Library for finding me images for the book so speedily. I would like to express my gratitude to Sue Morgan for advice given, Jean Holder for patiently reading revisions of the script and Eleanor Tagliarini for proofreading the script. I am grateful to the anonymous readers for their helpful comments. Finally, I would like to thank Emma Goode, Emily Drewe and Beatriz Lopez at Bloomsbury for their support and kind words. All errors and omissions in the text are entirely my own.

Abbreviations and conversions

Abbreviations

NSL   *New Survey of London*
LCC   *London County Council*

Conversion table

Four farthings = one penny
Two half pennies = one penny
Twelve pennies = one shilling
Thirty pennies = half a crown
Two shillings and sixpence = half a crown
One Guinea = twenty-one shillings

Introduction

'**A**lthough a distinct "teenage" culture was to await the affluence of the years after the Second World War, there were manifestations of it before 1939'.[1] Thus stated Stevenson who pointed to the fact that 'young people could often find work more easily than adults'; he continued by stating that 'there was a large group of relatively affluent young people, without family responsibilities, who presented a market for clothes, mass entertainment and recreational opportunities of other kinds'.[2] Making reference to the late nineteenth and early twentieth centuries, Osgerby claimed the emergence of a 'discernable youth leisure market ... a response to the significant level of disposable income enjoyed by many working youngsters'.[3] These comments reflect the prevailing view that a teenage culture did not emerge in England until after the Second World War when youth had greater affluence. While Fowler has challenged this by shifting the time frame to the interwar years, he firmly made the case that the emergence of a teenage consumer culture was based upon levels of disposable income, mainly on the part of young lads.[4] Equating the advent of a teenage consumer culture with levels of disposable income became the accepted wisdom, so much so that it has been perpetuated by much of the research in the latter part of the twentieth century concerning the development of youth culture. However, this line of reasoning raises issues that need to be challenged: the acceptance of the view that a teenage consumer culture only emerged during the latter half of the twentieth century has been reinforced by a gender blindness in terms of the scant attention given to the ways in which girls experienced leisure. Their pursuit of leisure was very different to that of their brothers. This is despite Bailey stating 'there is a case to be made for women as leisure leaders in the interwar years'.[5] More specifically it will be argued that it was teenage working-class girls who were at the forefront of the commercial leisure culture; they did not wait until the post-Second World War era, they were embracing the emerging teenage leisure culture during the interwar years. Part of the reason for not acknowledging this is to be found in the lack of understanding of the potential of working-class culture to provide the capacity for young people to gain access to leisure during the interwar years rather than a dependence upon levels of income.

This book provides a timely reassessment of the advent of a teenage consumer culture by bringing the experiences of working-class girls to the foreground. The case will be made that attention needs to be refocused on the interwar period, when commercial leisure became popular across the country. It will be argued that the group of people who were best positioned to take up the leisure activities available were teenage girls. There will be a particular focus on working-class girls who were in demand as workers in areas of the country where new light industries and new production processes were developing. It will be argued that their creative use of the cultural practices used by the working classes on a day-to-day basis provided girls with the means to gain access to the leisure pursuits of their choice. Challenging previous assumptions that the development of a teenage consumer culture was based upon levels of disposable income, this book will instead focus on how girls drew upon their everyday cultural practices to gain access to the products of the burgeoning commercial leisure industry. Following this, it will demonstrate that for teenage girls leisure came to shape their identity by weaving the informal practices of their class culture with commercial leisure activities. It will also reveal how leisure acts as a cultural agent by investigating the fluidity of the inter-connections of class, gender, leisure and identity, exposing the tensions in the ways that femininity is constructed. This provides valuable insights into how leisure came to act as a means to rehearse and contest identity during the period and how subjectivity came to be defined via consumption rather than production.

Bringing girls to the foreground will redress the ways in which they have in the past been marginalized in the historiography of youth and leisure. From the late nineteenth century there developed an acknowledgement that youth was a definite stage in the life cycle and that it was differentiated along class and gender lines. It is ironic that, despite the suggestion that youth have been the subject of more moralizing and theorizing than any other group from the late nineteenth century,[6] it was only in the latter part of the twentieth century that youth became the focus of interest from historians.[7] This has arisen partly due to the assumption that for the majority of young people during the first half of the twentieth century there was no rite of passage from childhood to adulthood. Springhall, seeking to offer an explanation for the limited focus on adolescence generally by historians, suggested that the period of youth may have been neglected in research because age as a variable had not been seen as fundamental in the way that class, gender or ethnicity had in terms of their impact on social and political change.[8] While the emergence of a historiography of youth was to be welcomed, early work in this area mainly focused on the leisure of young boys and in doing so simply sought to negate the experiences of girls.[9] Despite many of those working in the field being aware of the omission of the experiences of girls, little was done to rectify this.[10] Ironically, Hendrick's *Images of Youth: Age Class and the Male Youth* simply refers the reader to Dyhouse[11] should they wish to explore the notion of adolescence in relation to girls.[12] Springhall first discusses the phenomenon of adolescence in a male context only and then, when talking of the club movement that sought to shape the leisure of working-class youth, he does so in the context of boys' youth clubs rather than include an account of club provision for girls. Nor does he explore the implications of the debates that took place throughout the interwar years about the possibilities and potential of developing mixed clubs.[13] Humphries makes use of girls' accounts of their experiences, but does not explore fully the implications related to issues of social control and gender.[14] The gender blindness inherent in this work allowed Springhall to refer to the absence of girls from leisure and street corner society,[15] which was far from the case as demonstrated throughout the interwar years in the concerns of the Girls' Club movement about the lifestyle of teenage girls. The marginalization of girls in the development of youth culture was symptomatic of the limited significance of women in the development of cultural formations. However, in a move to bring the leisure experiences of girls to the foreground in more recent research,[16] what becomes clear is the need to challenge perceived assumptions about how individuals experience the world they inhabit and, as a consequence, how this impacts upon their subjectivity and their understanding of their place in the world. Locating the girl in the background has been consistent in the historiography of the development of youth culture until relatively recently, yet the lifestyle of girls during the interwar period would suggest the need to rethink their place in the development of youth culture and challenge why they have been located in the background. Understanding the nature and symbolic meaning of teenage working-class girls' leisure will allow the experience of being a woman to be explored at a specific stage in the life cycle when she did not have the responsibilities that she would take on when becoming a wife and mother. By broadening the scope of analysis to include aspects of women's lives outside of their domestic role, and focusing on a stage in the life cycle when their responsibilities in this area were fewer, will allow a different perspective of girls' lives to be foregrounded.

This book relocates the emergence of the teenager to the interwar years, and in doing so the argument will be made that during this period there was a nascent teenage consumer culture emerging in England that was centred upon the use of leisure. Drawing upon Bailey's comment that 'the history of women in leisure is slowly being recovered',[17] and his observation that 'working-class girls embraced successive dance crazes with the eagerness boys of their class reserved for sport',[18] the case will be made for an alternative reading of the development of a teenage consumer culture that brings girls to the foreground as key participants in the consumption of commercial leisure during the interwar period. The case will also be made that it was the gendered nature of identity that rendered the experiences of girls as invisible in the past. Equally, the assumption that levels of disposable income were a key factor in the emergence of a teenage consumer culture are problematic too. The term 'teenager' was one that was in use during the 1920s, but more so in the 1930s. The social attributes associated with the teenagers of the 1950s and 1960s were in evidence during the interwar period, so much so, that it could readily be argued that there was an emerging youth culture in ways similar to that of the early post–Second World War decades. Indeed, a number of historians have acknowledged that aspects of a teenage way of life can be identified pre-1939.[19] It will be argued that what was different during the interwar period was that girls were at the forefront of the movement. Another distinctive feature was that they asserted their entitlement to be part of the new consumer culture. It would be useful at this point to clarify the age range of the girls who are the focus of this study. It would seem that in discussing the lives of teenagers, reference is being made to young people between the ages of thirteen to nineteen, and while this might technically be the age range being referred to, it does not always relate to significant moments in the lives of young people. For example, the significant point in the lives of young people during the interwar years was the age of fourteen when the majority of young people left school. Fowler defines teenagers as those who were wage earners between the ages of fourteen and twenty-one when they would have completed their apprenticeships.[20] Abrams suggested that the teenage years were between the time they left school to the time they married.[21] 'Juvenile' is a term that was widely used when making reference to those aged fourteen to seventeen. While the term was popular with social commentators by the end of the period the term 'youth' was more widely used to describe those between the age of fourteen and the age that they married. The age at which girls were entitled to an adult wage was eighteen in most industrial and clerical jobs; young men qualified for a youth rate at the age of nineteen and an adult rate at the age of twenty-one. This study will explore the lifestyle of girls between the ages of thirteen and twenty.

Much of the expanding leisure provision during the interwar years was aimed at young people, and a number of studies have confirmed that it was young girls who were prominent in the consumption of newer forms of leisure such as dancing and the cinema.[22] Despite the marginalization of the leisure experiences of girls until recently in the historiography of youth and leisure, there is nonetheless a rich vein of material to draw upon in order to gain some understanding of how girls were understood at that historical moment. Working-class girls are the specific focus of this study, but it is important to remember that class and gender are just two constituents of identity. As Giles has suggested, women's experience, identity and meanings of their status are shaped and understood by their class, age and the historical moment.[23]

In this instance, what becomes clear is that when drawing upon evidence about youth culture, there is a problem, as Dyhouse noted, of interpreting sources that have been written in a specific ideological framework,[24] but also there is clearly a problem of the interpreter accepting ideological assumptions upon which images were socially constructed in the past. The journals from the Girls' Club movement have been a very useful resource not only in terms of drawing attention to the reactions to girls' choice of leisure but also in recognition that various reports were written with a particular audience in mind; very often, reports and articles were pitched at an audience who might support their work with the donation of funds. The journals of the different organizations provide a valuable insight into the subtle differences in the ways in which they organized leisure for girls. They also present ample evidence of girls participating in a range of leisure activities offered by the numerous clubs or other forms of organized leisure such as the Girl Guides and the Girls' Life Brigade. These organizations had a very clear understanding of what leisure should consist and its purpose. As this book will reveal, their interpretation of what leisure should be did not always accord with how girls wanted to spend their leisure time. Contemporary newspapers have proved of great value in gauging the reactions to the ways that girls engaged in leisure and adopted the image of the modern girl. Articles and commentaries in local and national newspapers present evidence of girls' leisure pursuits creating tensions concerning femininity. Drawing upon the everyday cultural practices of working-class girls, the book explores the mechanisms they used to gain access to the fashionable dress, films, music and dances of the day. It reveals their persistence and ingenuity to be part of the new commercial leisure culture.

In order to explore how girls drew upon their own class cultural practices, oral testimony of those growing up in the period has been used. All the women interviewed for this study had grown up in Bermondsey and many of them still lived in the area. It must be made clear that conducting interviews with those who grew up in Bermondsey during the interwar years does not simply produce an account of things that happened in the past. Memories that are narrated are more complex than simply a recall of what happened, they are inter-woven over the years with public memories and as such they are always contingent.[25] When the women recalled events from their teenage years, they would often compare their youthful experiences with those of young girls today, commenting on how harsh their lives had been in comparison with contemporary teenagers. It is also useful to be mindful of the issues raised by Borland concerning the way that narratives can be interpreted by the researcher in ways that can misrepresent what the interviewee has said.[26] It is important that the narratives provided by the women in this study are not viewed as an essential truth; the women are in fact recollecting through the prism of time and layers of experience and their accounts are also articulated in the context of their present experiences. Within the field of leisure history, a number of studies have sought to give an overview of the development of leisure during the interwar period.[27] Although these are useful, there is a need to focus on the micro level as well in order to gain more than a generalized view about the impact of the development of leisure. Such an approach will highlight the diverse ways that it was experienced; for example, while studies like that of Jones[28] give an excellent overview of the leisure pursuits of the working class generally, there is also a need to concentrate on regional variations in the ways that the working classes made use of leisure. Walvin and Walton pointed out that many areas of the history of leisure had remained unexplored particularly in the context of regional studies. They argue that by shifting the focus to local studies, previously neglected themes could be highlighted.[29] Acknowledging this as well as exploring the issues on a national level, this study will also focus on a particular locality, in this case Bermondsey in south-east London. This will enable the nuances of the material nature of class culture to be taken into account. Women might have said in retrospect that they had no time for leisure, but the teenage girls of the 1920s and 1930s made the point that leisure was for everyone, not just certain sections of society.

1

Setting the scene

In 1937, having completed his journey around England, Priestley reflected upon the differences he had observed in various parts of the country and concluded that he had 'seen lots of Englands'.[1] He described what he called the new post-war England: 'This is the England of arterial and by-pass roads, of filling stations and factories that look like exhibition buildings, of giant cinemas and dance-halls and cafes, bungalows with tiny garages, cocktail bars, Woolworths, motor-coaches, wireless, hiking, factory girls looking like actresses, grey-hound racing and dirt tracks, swimming pools....'[2] Priestley's description of the new post-war England reveals a world that was very different to that which existed only a few years earlier, yet it does to a certain extent epitomize much of what was new during the interwar period. While not every aspect of this 'new' England was to be found in all parts of the country, it was, however, a landscape that girls growing up came to recognize and, in many respects, they became part of what it represented. Two particular features of this 'new' England had a significant impact on the lives of working-class girls and in some respects were responsible for bringing them to the foreground during the interwar years. The first was the changing nature of the production process in some industries that employed large numbers of teenage girls. The second was the expansion of commercial leisure that became increasingly accessible during the period. Significantly, the latter caught girls' attention at a time when there was a growing expectation of an entitlement to some leisure. To make clear how these changes interlinked and the extent to which they had an impact on the lives of working-class girls, it is useful to contextualize how the new post-war world awakened girls to the possibility of a different lifestyle to that experienced by the older generation in terms of work and leisure. For girls, it was a time of change when social mores were challenged on their part; many of them smoked, wore make-up, cut their hair short, wore shorter skirts and dresses: their new look made people notice them. Their style powerfully signified that they were different to the older generation and that they were part of a changing world. Girls growing up during this period were increasingly aware that they had the opportunity to be consumers as well as producers, and as such they were positioned to make choices about the leisure they pursued. In order to explore the extent to which socio-economic conditions impacted on their ability to engage in leisure, it is useful to move away from broad generalized observations about work, leisure and identity across the country and instead focus on a specific locality so that consideration can be given to the nuanced nature of material conditions and the extent to which the nature and type of work impacted on the leisure activities of teenage girls which in turn influenced their identity.

Reference to the period often evokes images of the dire poverty experienced in areas of the country blighted by economic depression. Hunger marches, dole queues and the general strike are vivid images that have come to define the interwar years.[3] Certainly, unemployment was a significant feature that fluctuated throughout the period. It was more acute in some areas than others, as those living in South Wales and the north of England, for example, experienced long-term unemployment due to these areas being dependent upon heavy industries such as coal-mining, ship-building, textiles and steel, all of which experienced a decline during the period. The impact of this economic downturn resulted in a great deal of poverty that was felt by those living in these parts of the country, and in many respects this came to define the interwar years. But it is important to acknowledge that this did not reflect conditions across the whole of the country and the high levels of unemployment that were to be found in specific geographical locations need to be put into perspective; for example, in the 1920s, 70 per cent of all unemployed people came from only nine counties.[4] Clearly, this suggests that the experience of growing up during this period would have been profoundly different depending on geographical location. Yet despite regional variations in levels of unemployment, there would have been some commonality of experience across the country. For example, it was observed that if young people lost their job, they were more likely to gain another job easily.[5] In relation to the employment levels of youth generally, Bourke has suggested that boys of a particular age were positioned to have some upward social mobility whereas girls were more likely to be in part-time work which was not protected by unemployment legislation.[6] Interestingly, what had a positive impact on the quality of the lives of some girls was what was seen to be a paradox in the economy during this period, in that while there was a contraction of old established staple industries, there was major economic growth in some areas of the country and as a consequence there was a rise in the standard of living for the majority of the population by the end of the period.[7] It is this anomaly that draws attention to the usefulness of focusing on particular localities to determine the subtleties of the economic landscape and how they impact on changes in the nature of social and cultural life. This draws attention to how the nature of employment was gender specific across the life cycle with women generally being perceived as secondary in the labour market as their primary role was firmly located in the domestic sphere. This would have been a powerful subliminal message that girls growing up would have received.

An important development within the period that had an impact nationally was the creation of the Central Electricity Board in 1926 that enabled the development of modern power stations and a national grid to transmit electricity. The ramifications of this were profound in terms of the potential to change the nature of production in industry and, as a consequence, improve the quality of people's lives. Electricity made it possible to produce a wider range of consumer goods in relation to not only the production process but also the variety of domestic appliances that became available. However, it did more than this; it allowed the development of the cinema, the wireless and transport of various forms, all of which had the potential to provide people across the social class spectrum with the opportunities to broaden their horizons. By the end of the period, electricity had also played a major part in the establishment of a motor car industry in England. Equally, the development of plastics, rayon and artificial fibres that were increasingly used in the clothing industries also fostered industrial growth. Possibly the most radical change that allowed the expansion of industry was the use of electricity in the production process in that it enabled the introduction of the assembly line in some industries that transformed production by speeding up the process, thus increasing output capacity. Many companies such as Peek Frean in Bermondsey made use of the time and motion production line that controlled the levels of output. A major outcome of the new production processes was that they provided an increase in job opportunities for young girls and as the period progressed some girls were also in demand for clerical posts and shop work.[8] The mass production for a consumer market that took place during the interwar years also had a knock-on effect in terms of the development of the advertising industry. Magazines, the cinema and billboards were all used to advertise the latest consumer goods that were being produced. As the period progressed, gimmicks such as free gifts were used to entice consumers to purchase more.[9] There were also changes in the retail industry with the growth of the chain store that altered the experience of shopping and made a wider range of consumer goods available.

Priestley's idea of 'lots of Englands' was an apt description of the impact of the economic changes taking place throughout the 1920s and 1930s. His observations about the differences in terms of the quality of the lives of people he had met on his journey reflect the stark contrast between these lives in different parts of the country. It is true that, as the period progressed, growing levels of economic success were to be found in some parts of the country as a result of the establishment of new light industries that flourished in the Midlands and certain areas in and around London and the south of England. These industries benefited from technical advances in food processing, light engineering, and the manufacture of electrical appliances such as washing machines, radios, gramophones and electric cookers, so much so that the arterial roads around London with their art deco factories came to symbolize modernity and a new economic structure that was being established via the industries that were housed in these factories.[10] Perceptions of the interwar period often conjure up a simplistic view of a North–South divide, but the situation was more complex. Beddoe, for example, has firmly made the case for an economic North–South divide during the period.[11] While she is correct to set out the stark economic differences between parts of the country, images of the North–South divide are problematic in that they are generalized and therefore do not allow for an acknowledgement of the diversity of the economy within regions. Towns and cities had their own particular circumstances that would have influenced the quality of life of those residing there. Within towns and cities, conditions would have differed depending upon the locality with certain streets or areas being deemed better than others. Reinforcing this, Tebbutt has rightly drawn attention to the differences in experience of those living in Nottingham and those in other areas of the north of England.[12] Similarly, rural areas would have felt the impact of economic conditions in ways that were different to those in towns and cities. This reinforces the need to focus on specific localities within regions in order to facilitate an understanding of the impact of local economies on the nature of leisure. Equally, it is vital to acknowledge the impact of class and gender on the individual in terms of how he or she experiences the world. Utilizing the concept of social class to define the individual, it is important to realize that social classes are not homogeneous groups, they are comprised of people with different aspirations and expectations, and as individuals they experience the nature of class in ways that are pertinent to them and are influenced by their surroundings. In the same manner, gender is an important constituent of identity which influences and is influenced by the material conditions of the individual's experience. This underlines the value of focusing on the day-to-day lives of people in order to explore the impact of localized socio-economic conditions on the quality of their lives. This would enable a more subtle approach to exploring what girls' experiences were in different parts of the country that impacted on their experience of leisure.

A useful illustration of how these nuances in material circumstances impacted on those who lived within relatively close proximity to one another is to be found in London. Images of England at this time invariably depict London as having a flourishing economy with very little poverty – in part because of the impact of the new light industries. But this generalization is not helpful as it does not depict the reality. A significant feature of the London labour market was that, unlike many other areas of the country, it was not dependent on one major industry as a form of employment. London, therefore, did not experience the structural long-term unemployment that was present in some other parts of the country. Unemployment was more likely to be intermittent with the levels varying greatly between London boroughs. Although it was one of the main manufacturing areas of the country during this period, London could have been likened to a series of small towns each with their own specific industries that clearly influenced the nature of work and the experience of gaining work in different areas of London.[13] Even though it did have some heavy industry, at the beginning of the period much of the industry was comprised of small workshops that specialized in the manufacture of particular products such as clothes in various part of London, clocks in Finsbury, furniture in Shoreditch and tailoring in Tower Hamlets and Bermondsey. Each part of London seemed to have a particular specialism; for example, Jerry White talked of the way that the increase in production of electrical products throughout the interwar years impacted on the nature of employment for those living in Campbell Bunk in north London,[14] yet this had little impact on Bermondsey in south-east London, just a few miles away. The diversity of the local economies within London provides a valuable opportunity to explore how the nature of employment within a specific area would have impacted on the material conditions of girls' lives and, in doing so, the extent to which work shaped their leisure. Focusing on a specific location therefore provides an opportunity to explore the impact of distinct local economies on the day-to-day lives of girls. Bermondsey provides an excellent example of this in part because of the nature of the industry in the locality that defined the lives of those who lived there.

Despite the quality of life improving for many people by the end of the period, the experience of poverty was still very real in some areas. Social surveys provide evidence of significant numbers in poverty.[15] Evidence from *The New Survey of London Life and Labour* (hereafter NSL) reinforced the extent of the differences within London; for example, 17.5 per cent of the population were living in poverty in Bermondsey, exceeded by only three other boroughs in the eastern area of London (the borough with the highest number being Poplar with 24 per cent of the population experiencing poverty).[16] Conversely, in the Borough of Lewisham, a few miles away from Bermondsey, only 4.8 per cent of the population were living in poverty.[17] These differing figures from boroughs that are in relatively close proximity illustrate clearly that there is a need to move away from a big picture of regional experience and to focus instead on a microlevel and concentrate on the locality in order to understand how localized conditions shaped individual identity.

The causes of this persistent poverty in Bermondsey were due to a number of factors: the nature of employment, the rate of unemployment, low wages in many industries and poor housing. The NSL also drew attention to the persistent housing shortage in the borough, noting that Bermondsey had one of the highest levels of overcrowding in the whole of London.[18] The shortage of housing was reflected in the rents charged. Dr Connan, the medical officer of health in Bermondsey, stated in an article in *The London Evening Standard* that rents in Bermondsey ranged from 5 shillings for one room to 35 shillings a week for six rooms. In contrast, he estimated the average weekly wage in the borough to be between £2 2d. and £2 5d.[19] The causes of persistent poverty were complex; rather than a lack of employment, inadequate levels of income were seen as the cause.[20] Poverty was particularly felt in areas where the Board of Trade did not include smaller units in their scope of agreement regarding conditions of pay, Bermondsey being one such area where this occurred and it would have been girls and women who were most likely to work in these smaller units. Like other areas of the country, the nature of the work in Bermondsey influenced the quality of the lives of those living in the area. Writing in the *Bermondsey Labour Magazine* in April 1920, Dr Alfred Salter, justice of the peace and parliamentary candidate for West Bermondsey, described it as 'not a nice place to live in. The air is thick and sooty. The smells are – well they are! The streets are dingy and grey. The houses are small and pokey. ... The people are herded and huddled together – overcrowded per room, overcrowded per house, overcrowded per acre....'[21] While he could have been writing about many urban areas around the country, the smells he made reference to were of particular significance in the lives of teenage girls who grew up in the area. In his survey of London in the late nineteenth century, Booth stated that Bermondsey had its own peculiarities regarding socio-economic conditions.[22] These 'peculiarities' related to the nature of the industry in the area. The local economy had been determined by the fact that it had the river Thames as a boundary on the north and east side, giving three-and-a-half miles of water frontage. The fact that it was next to the Port of London meant that with the building of the docks in the nineteenth century it became a thriving industrial area, processing and distributing much of the food brought into the Port of London. Indeed, it was known as the larder of London. According to evidence gathered by London County Council (hereafter LCC) at the time of the 1921 Census, ninety-one people described themselves as dock labourers for every thousand occupied males living in the borough, while another forty-eight per thousand were employed on the water as seamen, bargemen, boatmen and pilots.[23] Like other areas of the country, working in the docks was notoriously unreliable and poorly paid; the work was often casual with men only getting perhaps two days' work in a week. The fluctuations in the dock industry had a knock-on effect on those riverside industries that processed the goods arriving in the docks, with the result of increasing the precarious nature of employment for a broader group of workers other than the dockers themselves; indeed, quite often it could impact on a number of members of the same family. By 1932, the unemployment rate in Bermondsey was 17.8 per cent, which was 5 per cent more than the average in London. This was significant in that it clearly had an impact on family income and has become a powerful memory for those who grew up in the area: 'Father was a docker – that is whenever he could find work. He used to shape up at Hay's Wharf at eight o'clock every morning, but often he was never called on, so then he'd go home, get out his barra and go round the streets selling this and that.'[24] Traditional industries in Bermondsey varied and included tanneries, tin-box making, the clothing trades, biscuit and jam-making and other food-processing industries, soap manufacturing, perfume factories and ice cream factories. Recalling the pungent smells in the area, Clara noted:

> You could smell the jam, chocolate, the biscuits, the scent factory in Southwark Park Road, the pickle factory, the leather factory, and the Alaska fur factory. If you went down the Blue Anchor you say ... they're doing the jam today and then the jelly factory. ... There used to be Pearce and Duff in Rouel Road the custard factory and at Tower Bridge you had the vinegar factory.[25]

While the intensity and the range of smells might have been the norm for those who grew up in the area, they also denoted the diversity of industry that Booth alluded to when talking of the socio-economic peculiarities. As well as large companies locating their factories in the area, there were many smaller outlets that often employed men and women on a casual basis. The NSL indicated that the casual and intermittent nature of work had always been a central feature of the London labour market generally and was particularly so in Bermondsey.[26] Ironically, it was partly because of this that women and especially teenage girls fared relatively well in terms of gaining employment. They were also in demand because of the unskilled nature of the work and the low rates of pay as confirmed by oral evidence: 'women went from one job to another because it was low paid. The Alaska fur factory was possibly better paid, but again, it was relative for what they did and the stuff they were breathing in all the time.'[27] By the interwar period, the chief occupations for girls locally were to be found in the clothing trades, biscuit and jam-making or other food-processing industries. It was factory work which dominated the area, as Lil noted: 'Living in Bermondsey as I did you couldn't help noticing all the factories. They were everywhere around. You tended to think that the whole world was like this.'[28] Girls who worked in this area would have felt the impact of the new production processes of the assembly line that had implications for the nature of their working patterns. Davies, in his excellent account of working-class women's leisure, has drawn attention to the constraints upon women due to their structural position within the home as wives and mothers.[29] This is borne out by the detailed pen portraits given by women living in Bermondsey about their daily routines of housework and caring for the family on a meagre sum of money.[30] There was clearly very little time in their lives to participate in leisure activities outside of the home, and while this can provide a rich source of material to challenge what constitutes leisure,[31] it is also suggestive of the need to consider women's experience of leisure at a point when they were not constrained in this way. It is useful, therefore, to explore how the daughters of these women experienced leisure and what it meant for them at a period in their lives when they had some relative freedom. This is particularly apposite in relation to the analysis of women's leisure during the interwar years; concentrating upon this particular moment in women's lives will allow for an analysis of their leisure at a time when opportunities to engage in leisure external to the domestic environment were optimal. Girls would have been acutely aware of the changing nature of the work processes and the consequent implications for their own job opportunities, and they would also have realized that, while the new work processes improved their chances of gaining employment, they might not have increased their levels of pay. Girls were patently aware that their ability to gain work would have impacted on their access to leisure.

The interwar years witnessed an increased intervention on the part of government agencies into the lives of young people. Policies related to youth were both class- and gender-specific with a clear focus on preparing girls for their future roles as wives and mothers. The Education Act of 1918 raised the school leaving age to fourteen, which for most working-class girls was the age that they left school as very few could afford to stay on in education. The majority of working-class girls would have attended elementary schools that provided for those between the ages of five and fourteen, offering girls a curriculum of reading, writing, physical education, arithmetic and domestic subjects. For some girls there was the opportunity to go to the Central School that focused on developing their commercial or practical skills from the age of eleven, thereby enabling them to have a more vocational education and the possibility of greater job opportunities. For girls like Beatrice living in south-west London, the opportunity to attend the Central School increased her opportunities to gain a clerical job, which meant increased wages and a better quality of working life than her peers who did not have that opportunity.[32] Devereux contends that the increasingly literate population, due to the impact of compulsory education, meant a population that was receptive to education and its benefits;[33] however, this was not so for all people as there was not a culture of expanding educational horizons in the Borough of Bermondsey in terms of remaining in formal education. Lindsay noted that between 1914 and 1923, Bermondsey won 309 scholarships to county secondary schools, whereas Lewisham won 1,373 and Hackney won 1,489. Of the total scholarship winners in Bermondsey, 114 came from two particular schools, namely Keetons Road and Alma. Lindsay also noted that the children of general labourers were virtually absent from the scholarship lists.[34] The limited take-up of scholarships on the part of the working classes reinforces how their cultural norms and expectations were invariably determined by economic circumstances, so that the deferred benefits to be had from pursuing education were outweighed by the need to have money coming into the family home. For example, the Borough Road Polytechnic, a Trade school just outside the boundaries of Bermondsey, highlighted as a means of advertising the value of their courses and the long-term career prospects for those attending them. Yet economic factors would have overridden such long-term ambitions for many in the area, particularly as courses had to be paid for in advance.[35] Indeed, the priority for young people to work owing to the prevailing economic conditions was noted as a cause of lack of attendance at classes at the polytechnic.[36] What entry into the world of work meant for girls was that from the age of fourteen the majority of them took on a different status as workers. Specific legislation that was passed during this period would to some extent have had a subliminal impact on working-class girls in relation to shaping their lives. In 1918, the Representation of the People Act gave the vote to women over thirty years of age who fulfilled the property requirements or who had a degree. Subsequent legislation in 1928 meant that women between the ages of twenty-one and thirty were included in the entitlement to vote, and importantly the Act included working-class women. Women were granted the right to divorce on the same grounds as men in 1923 and in 1925 they gained equal guardianship of children and the entitlement to a widow's pension. The Sex Disqualification Act 1919 made it easier for women to go to university and to enter professions such as the civil service and teaching, but this was compromised as the marriage bar, which operated in these professions and indeed in some factories, often thwarted women who wanted to work after they were married. While very few working-class girls would have benefited from the latter Act, they would gradually throughout the period become aware of the wider employment opportunities for women at a time when they were able to engage in some of the leisure pursuits that their middle-class sisters pursued.

The policies implemented by local government also had the potential to play a role in determining the quality of peoples' lives. The political make-up of local government clearly influenced the material conditions of working-class families in many ways. London was governed by the LCC which was responsible for the overall governance of London; in 1900, it was divided into borough councils to take charge of local boroughs. Both the Bermondsey

Borough Council and the LCC were considered to be progressive forces during that period. In Bermondsey, it was the policies of the local Labour Party that attempted to provide the working classes, who comprised the majority of the population in the area, with a sense of self-respect. While their policies often focused on improving the quality of family life, in many respects it was teenage girls who felt their impact in that their policies enabled girls to gain some freedom from the domestic sphere. By 1934, the borough council was dominated by Labour councillors who were aware of the impoverished conditions that many residents experienced due to the nature of employment, poor pay, quality of housing and overcrowding. There was also recognition of a poverty of environment in terms of leisure facilities. The policies they introduced throughout the period may have been steeped in a sense of idealism, but they did seek to improve the quality of the lives of people living in the borough. The idealism on the part of the Labour Party was often impeded due to conflicting views about spending on the part of both national government and the LCC. The projects that the local authority funded provided some sections of the press with the opportunity to rail against the way that the local authority was spending money. 'Socialists Build a Hundred and Fifty Thousand Pound Palace of Baths' read one headline in the *Daily Mirror* in 1927. The article was drawing attention to the new ultra-modern baths that had been built in Bermondsey to allow those living there access to baths, as hardly anyone would have had one in their homes. The 'palace of baths' included vapour baths, two swimming pools (one first class and the other second class), 126 private baths and four baths for babies. It had marble halls and stained-glass windows.[37] While this made the headlines in a national newspaper, it was a typical development on the part of the local authority. What it did for girls growing up in the area was to provide them with some sense of dignity. It is something that women who grew up in Bermondsey at that time remember as an important part of their day-to-day lives: 'Used to go to have a bath once a week 'cos you didn't have baths at home.'[38] Recognizing the increasing value of the use of electricity in the home as the period progressed and the prohibitive cost of gaining access to electricity on the part of many of the local inhabitants, the local council offered free wiring, one shilling or one penny in the slot meters and fittings on hire purchase. This was advertised in the *Bermondsey Labour Magazine* that was circulated to all households.[39] Access to electricity would have benefited working-class families in that it enabled them to listen to a wireless powered in a more reliable way than the Crystal Set that often broke down. It also gave girls access to the latest music.

A key concern was providing facilities to improve the quality of health of people as this would have improved all aspects of the lives of working-class people. What is interesting is the results of the measures taken in Bermondsey to deal with health issues based upon the idea that prevention was better than cure. By 1901, Bermondsey had a full-time medical officer of health and by 1913 the council had employed health visitors and set up a baby class at the town hall. A maternity and welfare department was created which, by June 1924, had one full-time woman doctor, and was considering the need to employ another; it also had eight trained health visitors. The local council also funded five municipal maternity centres, and subsidized five voluntary centres.[40] It gained permission from the LCC that was responsible for education, to give health talks in elementary schools and it also had a health propaganda department that issued thousands of leaflets providing advice about health issues.[41] The first municipal solarium in Britain was opened in Bermondsey offering sunlight treatment for tuberculosis.[42] The council also licensed thirty-four dairy men in the borough to sell safe milk. It was also the first to open a municipal convalescent home in the country in 1924.[43] Other measures that the Labour administration implemented which had a positive impact on women specifically included free advice on health matters as well as cost price tickets for the necessitous to obtain free fresh milk.[44] Such was the success of these measures that in September 1924, figures show that Bermondsey had the lowest maternal death rate in any borough in London. Throughout the country there were 3.8 deaths of mothers per thousand confinements. Bermondsey in 1923 had 1.37 per thousand confinements,[45] and in 1935 it boasted no deaths of women in childbirth.[46] The setting up of these welfare services impacted on the quality of girls' lives in that some aspects of care were removed from the domain of the home, giving them the expectation of greater freedom in terms of not having to assist their mothers, and it also created an awareness on their part that their future role in the domestic sphere had the potential to be less pressured than their mother's generation. The new municipal laundry greatly improved the quality of life for women as these laundries enabled them to complete their washing much more quickly than they had previously been able to. This saving of time was particularly beneficial for teenage girls to whom the task of doing the washing often fell. For girls growing up in Bermondsey, it would have been the norm that there was access to medical care, bathing facilities and modern facilities to get the weekly wash completed. They might not have been explicitly aware at the time of the impact of these improvements, but they were nevertheless making a qualitative difference to the lives of teenage girls.

Girls had female role models of women in positions of authority with the high visibility of the middle class women who were actively involved in politics and held prominent positions on the local council. For example, by July 1922, it was noted that the West Bermondsey Women's Section had the highest number of women on public bodies.[47] In 1910, Ada Salter became the first woman councillor in London, and by 1939 Eveline Lowe had become the first woman Chair of the LCC. While these middle-class women were politically active in the area, their lives may have been seen on the part of young girls as somewhat distant from their own experiences. However, some girls would have had memories of women and girls walking out of Pinks, a local jam factory, in 1911 demanding more pay, as women and girls in other local factories followed suit. Dr Salter estimated that 14,000 girls were out on strike. The strikes resulted in companies agreeing to raise the wages of women and young girls. It was reported that at Pinks there was a pay rise of two shillings per week.[48] What would have registered with girls in a subliminal way was the message that they could assert themselves and make a difference. Lil recalled getting involved with the Aid for Spain campaign in her youth:

> I got involved with Aid for Spain that was when I was still with the mission group and the club and I thought this was the Christian thing to do was to collect food for these kids and so that's how I got involved with Aid for Spain. I had a couple of reasonable collections considering everybody was struggling anyway. I just asked the people in the mission to do it and bring it. I found out about Aid for Spain – there was a shop in Southwark Park Road down the Gomm gates it used to be a cats meat shop, man used to sell cats meat and they gave the window over to Aid for Spain and I was passing there one day and I saw this and I thought right that's what's got to be done.[49]

A major characteristic that came to define the interwar period was the boom in leisure activities that became available at a time when most workers experienced shorter working hours. Not only was there more time for leisure, but a greater choice of leisure activities came within reach of people across the social classes and in all parts of the country. This became an issue of debate throughout the period particularly in relation to the leisure pursuits of girls. By the beginning of the interwar period, the provision of leisure for working-class girls was well established by a range of voluntary organizations across the country. It included for example a variety of girls' clubs set up by philanthropic organizations and churches, the Girl Guides and the Girls Life Brigade. Early forms of leisure specifically for teenage girls had come under the auspices of organizations that had sought to carry out what Rooff termed 'social ambulance' work among young girls.[50] Some voluntary organizations used the term 'rescue work' to describe their aims of developing some self-reliance in girls and to inculcate within them religious morals at a time of rapid industrialization.[51] Although they aimed to offer guidance to working-class girls, these organizations did not necessarily have a commonality of aims or approaches to what they perceived to be the problems that girls faced. The mission settlement was a typical feature of the more impoverished areas of the urban environment. These settlements had been specifically set up to work with the poor, and often had links with major universities which provided both funding and students who wished to work at the settlement while taking time out from their studies. Given the socio-economic conditions in Bermondsey, it is hardly surprising that it was an area ripe for the development of all kinds of philanthropic work including the provision of leisure activities. Certainly, it was well provided for in terms of clubs for girls. This was confirmed by the NSL, which noted that all kinds of girls' social work were extremely well developed and that there were various sorts of clubs to suit all types in the borough.[52] It was also noted that 'The Settlements cater definitely for the rougher types, to whom neither the Church clubs nor the Evening Institutes in Bermondsey appeal.'[53] As well as the majority of churches having clubs attached to them, it was the settlements that were the main providers of philanthropic leisure in the area. There were three such settlements in Bermondsey that catered for girls: the Cambridge University Mission, the Bermondsey Settlement and Time and Talents which had been set up by the Young Women's Christian Association. Their attitudes to the causes and solutions to the poverty experienced by those living in the area provide an excellent example of how settlements, while having a common aim of helping to eradicate poverty, differed in the ways that this could be achieved. To illustrate this point, a comparison can be made between the aims of the Bermondsey Settlement and the Cambridge University Mission. When the Reverend H. D. Salmon founded the Cambridge University Mission in 1906, his solution to the problems he saw in the area was via the influence of religion and from the outset it was firmly stated that the mission was to be run on 'Evangelical principles and not social but religious lines'. Clarifying his objectives, he spoke of 'the mission, which has for its object the spiritual welfare of boys and girls in the neighbourhood of Bermondsey'.[54] While it was clear that the aims of the Cambridge University Mission were based upon a religious commitment, Dr Scott Lidgett, who founded the Bermondsey Settlement in 1891, was not so rigid in his doctrines. He made it clear at the outset that, although the aims of the settlement were Christian, they were non-sectarian in character. He listed the aims as follows: to increase Christian work, to become a centre for social life where all classes may meet together on equal terms, to enable men together to discuss general and special social evils and to seek their remedy, to take part in local administration and not to have any sectarian advantage.[55] An awareness of the links between poverty and how the poor spent their time when not working had underpinned the work of philanthropic organizations in areas like Bermondsey since the latter part of the nineteenth century. Certainly, it was an issue that influenced the motivation to provide clubs for the poor in the area. Reflecting upon the setting up of the Cambridge University Mission in Bermondsey in 1906, the Reverend H. D. Salmon spoke of having been struck by the poverty and squalor in the area where prize fighting, drunkenness, thieving, gambling and immorality abounded.[56] While he saw the problems arising from the type of leisure pursuit that working-class youth indulged in, the Reverend E. A. B. Royds, who was also associated with the Cambridge University Mission, pointed instead to the surroundings in which young people had to live as a causal factor of the problems. He argued that the problem in Bermondsey was not so much the fact of its socialism, or of its excessive drinking, or of its extreme and widespread poverty; it was rather a kind of collective evil arising out of the fact that there was little to uplift the spirit. The dull and monotonous life all around them had a depressing effect upon the young.[57] But this was about to change in relation to their leisure pursuits. During the interwar period, many girls preferred the newer forms of leisure which included cinema-going, dancing, listening to music and perhaps going to the greyhound stadiums or dog tracks that many towns had. A major issue that vexed many of the club leaders and was the subject of much discussion in their journals and at conferences was how the challenges from the rapidly growing commercial leisure sector could be dealt with. Llewellyn Smith noted that these organizations were moving away from the rescue-type work of their earlier days.[58] It is evident from the archives of the organizations that provided clubs for girls that they realized that they needed to reappraise their ideas about the purpose of the club in the wake of competition from the commercial leisure sector. In the NSL, Llewellyn Smith drew attention to the fact that it was recognized that workers had an entitlement to have time to engage in leisure pursuits. He observed that the average London worker had 'an increased margin of income, above that which is absorbed by bare necessities'.[59] He claimed that 'all forces at work are combining to shift the main centre of interest of a worker's life more and more from his daily work to his daily leisure'.[60] While not all Londoners would have experienced the rising rates of pay he spoke of, working-class teenage girls were able to go dancing and to the cinema and engage in leisure. This was the world that girls inhabited. Despite the poverty of their environment, they were able to see that the modern world was changing, there was more time for leisure and more leisure pursuits to choose from, and they became part of this.

2

'Leisure? What leisure?'

'Leisure? What leisure? We didn't have leisure in those days' is often the initial response from many working-class women who grew up during the interwar years when they are asked to recall their leisure activities during their youth. Their comment would seem to be affirmed by the dominance until relatively recently of a male focus in the historiography of the development of leisure in the twentieth century.[1] Yet there is a body of evidence to suggest otherwise; for example, the NSL noted that 'in 1931-1932 there were 258 cinemas in the County of London with a seating capacity of 344,000',[2] and it estimated that '70 per cent of the weekly audience consisted of girls and women'.[3] The popularity of the cinema with girls and women was not confined to London, as attested to by surveys carried out in other parts of the country during the interwar period.[4] Girls throughout the country frequented dance halls on a regular basis and learnt how to perfect the latest dances, they avidly listened to the latest music, they had a keen eye for the latest fashions, they joined organizations such as the Girl Guides and the Girls Life Brigade, they attended evening institutes and the various clubs set up by philanthropic organizations and they also actively participated in many sporting activities. Indeed, their leisure activities were the cause of much concern throughout the period. It is worth noting too that, during the period that the women were alluding to, the press almost became a conduit through which contemporary debates about leisure were played out; the newspapers consistently published reports from conferences and meetings that focused on leisure, thus reflecting its importance. There was also a constant flow of letters published in the press expressing concerns about how the expanding time for leisure should be spent and what constituted the right sort of leisure. These letters provide an insight into the ways that leisure was perceived at the time and make the comments of the women mentioned above all the more interesting. Given the public interest in leisure during the interwar years and the comments about not having any time for leisure in their youth on the part of those who grew up during the period, it is worth exploring how leisure has been constituted in the past and the present in ways that influence the subjectivity of the individual. The denial of having had time for leisure is particularly interesting in that following this comment, women invariably qualified the statement by pointing out that they had to work hard when they were younger. In doing so, they reveal how value judgements about work and leisure become internalized in ways that equate work with respectability while leisure is suggestive of not using time in an appropriate way. Their denial also reflects how they internalized the idea that to have time for leisure implied a lack of conformity in terms of notions of femininity that reinforced the idea that the role of women was to serve others rather than considering their own needs. Affirming that, ideologically, women were located in the home rather than in the public sphere[5] would also have impacted on how they understood their sense of self at that time and retrospectively, thus enabling them to deny that they had time for leisure. This reinforces the need to acknowledge that the concept of leisure cannot be understood in isolation.[6] It must be set in the context of the material conditions of the time that would have had an impact on how subjectivity was constructed.

Leisure became prominent in the lives of people and more specifically youth across the social class spectrum during the interwar period. It was also a time when a greater range of leisure opportunities became available to more people, which led historians to affirm that by the start of the interwar years modern leisure as we know it was firmly established in forms that can be recognized today.[7] Llewellyn Smith used the term 'leisure' in a broad sense 'to cover all that part of life which is not occupied in working'.[8] Clarke and Critcher reinforced the notion that leisure relied heavily on a contrast with work, perceiving leisure to be an escape from 'dull routine labour'.[9] They point out that 'leisure seems to offer the prospect of being things that work is not: the source of satisfactions, gratifications and pleasures'.[10] It has also been argued that leisure occurred in specific places and at specific times, so much so that Howkins and Lowerson argued that by the beginning of the twentieth century it would seem that the parameters between work and leisure had been well established.[11] It is these defining features of leisure that many of those working in the field have endorsed in the past, reinforcing the idea of the binary opposition of work and leisure. Defining leisure in this way is problematic in that it raises a number of questions about assumptions being made; the idea that work cannot provide satisfaction and that pleasure can is questionable, as what gives the individual pleasure is very personal and subjective. Although individuals might be engaged in manual labour that is not in itself pleasurable, the camaraderie that accompanies this labour might make it pleasurable. Indeed, some forms of manual labour might well give the individual satisfaction. Equally, defining leisure as that which is not work draws attention to the need to be clear about what constitutes work and whether it is the same for everyone. While it has been suggested that by the interwar period the parameters of work and leisure were clearly separated, this was not so for all groups of people. Fundamentally, defining leisure as that which is not work is problematic in that it does not take into account the gendered nature of how leisure is experienced. While the separation between work and leisure for men might seem clear, it is not so for women. For example, the boundaries between leisure and work for some women and teenage girls would have been far more amorphous for reasons related to the nature of their work within both the domestic and public sphere. To illustrate this, when working-class girls left school aged fourteen, they immediately entered the world of work, and when they married many of them still worked outside of the home as well as carrying out all of their duties within the home as wives and mothers. Countless women worked for pay as cleaners and cooks outside of the home; when they arrived home they would carry out the same tasks in the domestic sphere but this did not constitute work. Clearly, the work–leisure paradigm is not a helpful tool when trying to explore the nature of the meaning of leisure for women at all stages of the life cycle. The complexity of defining leisure raises a number of issues in terms of exploring the leisure experiences of women; first, it would seem that once faced with the responsibilities of home and family, women's opportunities for leisure outside of the home were limited. Davies, for example, claimed that it was harder for women to find the time for leisure because of the role they were expected to take on in the domestic sphere.[12] This is reinforced by Elizabeth Roberts' observation that women were expected to put the needs of their families before their own.[13] However, these roles would have been more intensive at certain points in their lives than others and different factors would have determined the extent and nature of their leisure partly based upon their social class. Housewives and mothers who were interviewed by Spring Rice revealed how the quality of life of a housewife was often determined to a great extent by the number of children she had and their ages,[14] which would clearly impact on the extent to which she could have time for leisure. Many of the women living in Bermondsey who were interviewed by Llewellyn Smith suggested that the quality of their leisure was influenced by the extent to which their husband was able to find work.[15] Women's role in the domestic sphere draws attention to the need for women to be recognized as experiencing the world in different ways according to the stage in the life cycle. What becomes clear is that rather than assuming a sense of universality of experience based upon gender or indeed class, it should be acknowledged that leisure is experienced in a diversity of ways. Acknowledging this will allow the pre-figured location of women as wives and mothers to be challenged in that it will enable women to be seen as actors in their own right who, at specific stages of the life cycle, take on different roles which impact on the nature of the leisure that they experience. This will allow for an exploration of what these roles meant at different stages of the life cycle and how they impacted on women's choice of leisure. It suggests the need for a more constructive framework within which to determine what constitutes leisure and the degree to which the definition of leisure is flexible in relation to class, gender, age and historical moment. It would seem clear that the conceptualization of leisure as that which is not work reinforces the need to rethink the work–leisure paradigm as it is clearly more complex than initially thought, especially in terms of women's experience of leisure. Ironically, in spite of the problematic nature of defining leisure in relation to work, it has until relatively recently provided the framework for much of the research into the history of leisure. As a result, research has tended to concentrate on institutionalized leisure, which, by its nature, focused on the male domain, thus reinforcing the assumptions that women did not have any leisure.[16]

What is required is a framework that acknowledges the complexity of defining leisure and celebrates the potential this has to open up debates that provide the capacity to understand more fully the multiplicity of meanings that leisure might have. It also enables assumptions about stereotypical behaviour based upon gender and class across the life cycle to be challenged and also allows for an understanding of the context of leisure activities. To illustrate this, while middle- and upper-class women invited friends for afternoon tea that involved conversation and sociability, for working-class women sociability might well be comprised of spending time having a gossip while hanging out the washing. The women were, to all intents and purposes, engaged in the same activity but in different settings. Fundamentally, it seems that the limitations of the work–leisure dichotomy, which have informed much of the history of leisure, are suggestive of the need for alternative frameworks which embrace a much more fluid understanding of what constitutes leisure. It becomes clear that conventional models of conceptualizing leisure are not helpful for understanding how women generally and more specifically teenage girls experienced leisure and the meaning it provided for them. Langhamer has quite correctly affirmed this, suggesting that the historiography of leisure does not provide the conceptual tools to explore the meaning of leisure for women.[17] Hill has usefully suggested that rather than focus on leisure simply as a series of activities, it is much more meaningful to perceive it as a process, which in itself has 'a determining influence over people's lives'. He makes the case that it has 'a pervasive influence', arguing that it is the practices and text of leisure that act as cultural agencies with the power to influence the individual consumer of leisure ideologically.[18] Leisure, therefore, is a process from which meaning is derived and leisure activities are inscribed in ways of thinking and behaving which contribute to how individuals see themselves and others. In doing so, this enables individuals to make sense of their social relationships. This is a far more helpful definition of what leisure is as it allows for a more fluid approach to understanding leisure. It provides the capacity to explore the meaning of leisure for women across the stages of the life cycle as well as enabling a consideration of the extent to which it influences identity. What it does affirm is that leisure is different for men and women[19] and as such requires an alternative framework within which to explore women's leisure. Following Wearing, the position will be taken that 'no one theory has all the explanations for human behaviour or human selfhood'.[20] In doing so, it will allow for the leisure pursuits of girls to be understood in the context of a sense of flexibility, acknowledging that individuals do not neatly fit into categorization. During the latter part of the twentieth century, feminist research provided a growing critique of the conceptualization of leisure with a focus on the inherent definitional ambiguities that marginalized the leisure experiences of women.[21] In doing so, this body of research provided the impetus to re-conceptualize leisure within a much broader definition that allows for the exploration of women's experience of leisure in a more holistic way. Paramount to this work was a recognition that leisure is different for men and women and, as such, should not be treated in the same way in terms of analysis.[22] This acknowledgement opened up possibilities to pose questions that had the potential to challenge preconceived understandings of what constituted leisure. More specifically, it provided the scope to consider the meaning of leisure for women, and to recognize that the meaning is fluid and changes over time, and is influenced by how gender relations are constructed at any given moment. For example, Wearing has suggested that leisure can be distinguished by the meaning of the activity and not the form,[23] and this was crucial for teenage girls. Within the following chapters, the leisure pursuits of teenage girls will be explored in terms of the meaning they derived from their leisure activities, and also the meaning others made of their leisure.

Re-conceptualizing leisure crucially provides the opportunity to focus on the day-to-day experiences of women at different stages of the life cycle, thereby bringing them to the foreground, which is of value as it allows for a specific concentration on the experiences of teenage girls for whom leisure played a significant part in defining their identity. The case will be made that they were only able to gain access to many of the leisure pursuits of their choosing by drawing upon their day-to-day cultural practices. This focus has the latent power to develop an understanding of why girls engaged in youthful leisure in the way that they did and it endorses the view that leisure needs to be re-signified in such a way that recognizes the daily experience of women's lives.[24] In his review of leisure research, Bailey drew attention to the way that research had been focused on institutionalized leisure rather than the informal day to day.[25] It has been this emphasis in the past that has sought to reinforce the assumptions that women generally did not have any leisure. Therefore, understanding the meanings and events of the fabric of everyday life allows for an interrogation of the importance of leisure in the lives of teenage girls that was demonstrated in the ways that their leisure pursuits came to be seen as a problem during the interwar years. Another crucial element of the re-conceptualization of leisure was provided by Langhamer, who drew attention to what might seem a very simple, but pertinent question that needed to be asked: What did women consider leisure to be?[26] Langhamer found that the responses that women gave in answer to this question revealed a breadth of understanding of what individuals thought constituted leisure. They also acknowledged the ambiguous nature of defining leisure. Interestingly, the survey conducted by Spring Rice in the 1930s reveals similar understandings of what constituted leisure on the part of women.[27] What women consider leisure to be will reveal a richer understanding about what constitutes leisure and why it is of value to women at different stages of the life cycle. Following Hill's suggestion that leisure is a process will enable a better understanding of why women reflecting upon their youth deny having had any leisure as it will bring to the surface what they consider leisure to be and how leisure has often been viewed as an indulgence.

Wearing has suggested that 'leisure spaces' can provide the potential to 'resignify women's subjectivities so that they are no longer inferiorized'.[28] She suggests that physical and metaphorical leisure spaces can allow for resistance to subjectivities that are foisted upon women.[29] Leisure therefore means more than just physical space; it is about personal spaces that allow girls to become women in their own right, and to constitute subjectivities of their own making rather than those that were imposed upon them. Rethinking what constitutes leisure can provide the opportunity to understand it as a space where identity can be rehearsed in ways that allow teenage girls to draw upon a range of identities other than the stereotypical roles that locate them in the domestic sphere. During the interwar years, it was girls' visibility in public spaces that drew attention to their choice of how to spend their leisure time. Their resourcefulness in gaining access to identities they wanted to explore was in a sense their imagined space where they could rehearse who they wanted to be. If leisure is perceived as a site of personal choice it therefore implies that it has the potential to be a site for resistant behaviour via the opportunities for self-expression through leisure.[30] The concept of resistance is useful to draw upon as it enables dominant discourses about femininity and what is deemed appropriate behaviour at any given time to be challenged.

These were issues that became part of public debate concerning the leisure pursuits and lifestyles of young girls throughout the interwar period.

Drawing upon these insights will provide a much more fluid understanding of what constitutes leisure and as a consequence, a greater understanding of its potential to act as a cultural agent, in that it contributes to the ways in which individuals see themselves and make sense of their social relationships. It also provides the space to probe the extent to which its power to act as a cultural agent changes according to different stages of the life cycle when women in particular would in the past have had different priorities and responsibilities. It is useful to acknowledge the potential that these alternative approaches have for analysing the leisure of girls in that they allow questions to be asked that have the capacity to provide a richer understanding of the meaning and impact of leisure. By the latter part of the twentieth century, a body of research had begun to explore these ideas in relation to women's leisure.[31]

It is useful to highlight the importance of contextualizing what constitutes leisure as this draws attention to how leisure means different things in different settings. With this in mind, leisure is contextualized in terms of foregrounding women's leisure at a specific stage of the life cycle in order to develop an understanding of how girls drew upon the normative behaviour of their own class culture to gain access to the leisure of their choice. It is useful here to acknowledge that it has been suggested that there are multiple meanings for leisure.[32] For example, Green, Hebron and Woodward found that rather than leisure being perceived as fixed activities in specific spaces, many of the women in their study saw it as something different. They talked of being free, resting, relaxing, having a gossip; for them a priority of leisure was linked to the pleasure of having time for themselves. This is reflected in the language they use to describe leisure, demonstrating that for many women there is not a clear separation between work and leisure.[33] This is worth exploring in relation to the leisure pursuits of teenage girls.

Spring Rice suggested that 'leisure is a comparative term'.[34] Making reference to the impoverished nature of the lives of the wives and mothers in her research, she described leisure as 'anything which is slightly less arduous or gives a change of scene or occupation from the active hard work of the eight hours for which she has already been up'.[35] Many of the women in her study equated leisure with sitting down to do some sewing or knitting.[36] The women who Langhamer interviewed were clear that leisure meant very different things and defining it was somewhat nebulous. They spoke of the ways that some activities that might constitute work could also be seen as leisure; for example, ironing might also take place while they were listening to the radio, which was seen as a pleasurable activity.[37] Acknowledging that leisure is more than a series of activities suggests it also encompasses pleasure and meaning that can alter at different stages of the life cycle, thus emphasizing that context is therefore crucial in relation to understanding the meaning of leisure for different groups. This emphasis upon context draws attention to the need to consider the impact that social class has on both the form and process of leisure. While older women were developing a perception of leisure as pleasurable moments that they snatched, often taking them away from their roles as wives and mothers, it was different for teenage girls; for them, leisure played a crucial part in their lives but in different ways to that of older women. While there might have been some commonality with older women in terms of leisure being the snatching of some pleasurable moments, for many teenage girls who worked in factories those moments were snatched both during the working day and outside of their working lives. With the introduction of the production line in many large factories, music was often played over a tannoy in order to speed up the production process. From the companies' perspective this was purely functional in that girls worked to the speed of the music. Yet girls just saw it as a pleasure to be able to listen to music while they worked. Some girls working on the production line took pleasure from the banter with others throughout the day. The boundaries of work and leisure often became blurred in other ways; for example, girls who worked in the tailoring trade often made their own clothes at home and enjoyed the process of making clothes in order to be fashionable when they went out dancing. This suggests a need to consider the wider aspects of girls' lives in order to develop an understanding of how they experienced leisure. The realization during the interwar years that time for leisure was expanding and the nature of leisure was changing provoked much public debate about how the time for leisure should be spent. What became a focus of concern was whether young people were engaged in the right sort of leisure. By the interwar period, teenage girls were embracing the new leisure culture with gusto; however, it was their enthusiasm for the newer forms of leisure that prompted concerns on the part of those involved in providing what was termed 'rational recreation' and became a prominent theme in debates about stability in society. Ironically for teenage girls, their visible engagement with leisure provoked much debate about the purpose of leisure during the period.[38] Although Tinkler has made the case as to why girls became a cause for concern in relation to their leisure activities in the 1930s and 1940s, their leisure activities did in fact raise concerns throughout the earlier decade.[39] Indeed, there was a long trajectory of concern about the lifestyle of young girls. During the early twentieth century, the behaviour of working-class girls was thought to be the result of new employment patterns, state education, commercial leisure and the impact of war.

While time for leisure was perceived as being something that was good, what concerned social commentators was the importance of youth generally engaging in the 'right sort of leisure'. This was particularly so for the working classes who, it was felt, were not discerning enough to choose the right sort of leisure and therefore needed guidance. This was a theme of a national conference entitled 'The Leisure of the People' held in 1919 in the wake of post-war reconstruction. A speaker at the conference, Dr A. H. Norris, a member of the Juvenile Organizations Committee, emphasized the growing importance attached to the expectation of leisure by arguing that 'before long, the daily life of the adolescent will be roughly divided up into eight hours of work, eight hours of sleep, leaving the remaining eight hours for meals and leisure'.[40] The purpose of pointing to the amount of time available for leisure was to emphasize the need to ensure it took an appropriate form. An article entitled 'Work and Leisure' published in 1926 encapsulated this idea: 'Leisure is essential for body, mind and spirit. It may however, easily be abused and requires thought and careful organization if it is to be rightfully used.'[41] For teenage girls, the right sort of leisure was invariably set in the context of what Clarke and Critcher termed 'rational domesticity'.[42] However, it was the emphasis on forms of leisure that were based upon this idea of preparing girls for their role within the domestic sphere which became problematic as girls were rejecting this and instead were making their own decisions about how they wanted to spend their leisure time. It has been argued that there was an attempt during the period to construct the housewife as a homogeneous figure;[43] certainly, gender ideologies shaped the nature and meaning of girls' leisure and behaviour. The construction of specific ideals of womanhood through recreation reveals the ways that leisure acts as a cultural agent in reinforcing gendered identities. It has been suggested that culture is gender differentiated in such a way that men accommodate influences while women challenge them and force change,[44] and this needs to be considered when analysing girls' use of leisure. While Fowler has made the case for the growing visibility of youth cultures during the interwar period, there is clear evidence, as will be demonstrated in this work, that the dominant participants in the rapidly developing commercialized leisure industry were teenage girls more so than boys and as such were at the forefront of changing expectations of what leisure should consist of. As Parratt has pointed out, working-class women found resources and opportunities for leisure and more importantly took their pleasure as they chose.[45]

During the interwar years, working-class girls were in a position to make use of leisure in ways that their mothers' generation might not have been. Parratt points out that women's capacity to confound the ways in which gender shaped leisure arose from the possibility for leisure to resist and subvert, revealing the potential for leisure to become a site of social tension.[46] An indication of the recognition of the importance of leisure for young people was the publication in the mid-1930s of a national survey of the nature of leisure available to young girls. The National Council of Youth Clubs under the auspices of the Carnegie United Kingdom Trust published the results of the survey that, it was reported in the press, 'will be of great service to everyone concerned with the problem of girls and their leisure.' It stated that the author of the report spoke of opportunities for the wise use of leisure that should be available for all youth so that they are trained in a sense of responsibility.[47] Ensuring that girls engaged in the 'right' sort of leisure had long been an ongoing concern on the part of many providers of leisure for girls who were trying to stake a claim for determining what constituted appropriate leisure for working-class girls. Certainly, it underpinned a great deal of the work of the Girls' Club movement throughout the period and was the subject of ongoing debates in the public domain.[48] Paramount to the debates about the 'right' sort of leisure was an acknowledgement that leisure was 'a modern phenomenon which constituted a distinctive sphere of social life'.[49] While concerns about youth were not new, the focus on their leisure pursuits did reflect the growing significance of leisure as a prominent area of life. It was within this context that the leisure pursuits of young people came to be seen as problematic. As time for leisure increased across the social classes, so too did concerns about engaging in the right sort of leisure, which was firmly gender differentiated. There were, however, differences of opinion as to what the right sort of leisure should be. The intensity of these debates reinforces the complexity of defining leisure as well as acknowledging that leisure is a process that has the capacity to shape the individual.

An article in the *Girls' Club Journal* entitled 'Leisure and its Opportunities' noted: 'For the first time leisure in its popular meaning, is no longer a privilege but has become an economic necessity'; it went on to say, 'Clubs can teach how to use leisure time correctly.'[50] The idea of using leisure time 'correctly' became a contentious issue during the interwar years. It was one that was the subject of debate within the Girls' Club movement that had rapidly expanded to embrace a wide range of organizations and had become a prominent advocate of organized leisure for girls. One of the challenges it faced during the interwar years was that many clubs still perceived the right sort of leisure to be that which was deeply rooted in the moralistic philosophy that had been instrumental in the setting up of such bodies, yet it was one which was becoming increasingly outdated and girls were rejecting what they had to offer. By the interwar period, although teenage girls were much more visible in the public world of leisure, their leisure pursuits were often the subject of much scrutiny on the part of those who had very specific views about the purpose of leisure. The problem was that the leisure that girls wanted to pursue did not always accord with what others wanted them to do. Evidence from the journals of organizations that provided clubs for girls reveals tensions between what those running the clubs perceived leisure to be and what girls wanted it to be. Often, what was being challenged on the part of girls was an acceptance of what were considered to be old-fashioned notions of femininity. Their choices of how they made use of their time for leisure are suggestive of their resisting leisure that others wanted them to engage with. In doing so, they were examining and rejecting identities that they did not want. By the beginning of the interwar period, concerns about the lifestyles of young people were well established as a subject of public scrutiny. It is therefore useful to consider how this impacted on perceptions of the ways that girls experienced leisure. It has, for example, been suggested that there is a need to explore how leisure as a discourse intersected with discourses on adolescence within the context of concerns for social stability.[51] Certainly, the period was one in which there were concerns about young people in particular enjoying more unregulated leisure. Their use of time outside of work generally gained more attention in relation to perceiving the leisure pursuits of working-class youth as problematic. Their use of leisure became part of public debate and links were made between leisure and stability in society, the stability of social relations between the classes and the security of democracy.[52] In relation to teenage girls, these concerns focused on their future roles as wives and mothers.

A potential solution to the problem of ensuring that young people engaged in the right sort of leisure was thought to be in the provision of educative leisure. It was a major area within which government agencies sought to intervene in the lives of young people and serves to illustrate well the tensions inherent in leisure provision at that time. By the beginning of the twentieth century, there had been a rationalization in the administration and provision of education nationally, so that responsibility was in the hands of the local authorities. Given that the majority of young people left full-time education at the age of fourteen and therefore were no longer under what was considered the watchful eye of the authorities, evening classes were seen as a means to maintain some control and influence to guide them through adolescence. His Majesty's Inspectorate endorsed the positive effects of what was termed 'adult education', noting that it taught people how to use their leisure better and that it had a civilizing effect.[53] One of the most important agencies for adult education in London was the evening institute that aimed to provide for those who could not gain an education during the day. Specific institutes for women were set up which catered for what were considered women's needs. The curriculum offered was deemed to be non-vocational. Subjects were mainly domestic, laundry work, needlework, millinery, health and first aid, humane subjects and light physical exercise.[54] Interestingly, there was no age limit in the women's institutes as there was in the institutes for men. The classes sought to provide women and girls with skills that were perceived to be necessary to fit them for their future roles as wife and mother or for what was known as women's work. It is ironic to note that the NSL defined non-vocational education as a leisure pursuit, and saw it as the 'master key to all forms of self culture'.[55] Yet girls and women were not necessarily being encouraged to broaden their horizons outside of their stereotypical role of wife and mother. Ironically, in the same report, comment was made which showed that the least popular subjects at classes were cookery, health subjects, laundry work and domestic handwork.[56] Such observations confirm the lack of awareness on the part of the authorities about what those attending the institutes felt they needed. Inherent in the objectives of the institutes was an assumption that teenage girls had the same needs and desires as older women and also saw women only in the context of their domestic role. What is evident from the level of demand for such classes is that this clearly was not the case. The popularity of these classes as a form of leisure is difficult to determine accurately as classes took place at a number of different types of institution, not all of which kept detailed records. The reports from the different evening institutes suggest that the take-up of places was more positive in areas which were more affluent or where people were employed in skilled or professional occupations.[57] The reluctance to enrol on courses perhaps reflected the priority given to education over other forms of leisure on the part of those who could see some relevance to this improving leisure. Ironically, when the Bermondsey Settlement did set up a typing class that would have provided those attending with a broader range of skills to gain better-paid employment, it had thirty-four people register to attend the classes but only two typewriters. When the settlement was visited by inspectors from the LCC, the inspectors commented, 'The arrangements are altogether unsatisfactory.'[58] This observation was based upon not only the limited number of typewriters, but also the fact that the instructor was unqualified, knew little of modern methods of teaching typing and had been incapacitated in the left hand during the war and was therefore unable to demonstrate on a machine.[59] As well as classes being organized at centres specifically set up for adult education, those in charge of the evening institutes had to liaise with the missions and clubs which provided classes in an attempt to reach out to a wider audience. While these institutions were eager to support the promotion of education as a means of self-improvement, a culture clash often occurred between the clubs, which had been used to operating on somewhat flexible lines, and the increasingly bureaucratic education authorities which had a more formalized approach to their work with systems which had to be adhered to.

A perennial problem throughout the period for these classes was attendance. Bermondsey provides a good illustration of this. Funding formulas were such that attendance was a vital issue. Those in charge of education establishments were instructed that classes could only run once a certain number had enrolled. If the roll fell below the specified number, then the class was to close. From its opening, the Keetons Road Women's Institute in Bermondsey experienced the problem of fluctuations in attendance. The head teacher noted in the log book repeatedly that classes had to be closed due to the small numbers attending.[60] The rigour with which funding formulas were implemented also meant that in response to an inspection report, Miss Callender, a member of the Bermondsey Settlement Education Committee, had to plead to inspectors for mitigating circumstances in the hope that grants would not be cut.[61] She drew attention to the fact that within the local area the late hours of work meant that many arrived at the classes too late to register. The consequence of low numbers can be seen in the case of an embroidery class at Dockhead in Bermondsey that was closed after only twelve lessons in January 1920.[62] Ironically, this uncertainty about potential class closure could have led to a reluctance to enrol in courses which might not run for more than a few weeks. It is ironic that the rationalization and accountability imposed by the LCC, which was in overall charge of education, effectively reduced the provision it sought to encourage. Although the small take-up of some subjects might suggest an unrealistic view as to what would be appropriate in the area on the part of those planning the provision, the case can be made that class closure could be construed as a lack of flexibility on the part of the authorities which did not take into account the fluctuations in local economic conditions and the need for longer-term strategies to encourage attendance. To look more closely at the importance of attendance, the figures at the Bermondsey, Rotherhithe and Fair Street Institutes show that there was not a great increase in attendance during the 1920s; in fact there was at one point a fall in numbers.[63] Evidence also confirms that the majority of those attending were of a younger age, which suggests that ties of officialdom became weaker as teenage girls got older and the relevance of education seemed less important.[64] Similarly, the figures for the Keetons Road Institute confirm that on the whole, more girls attended classes at a younger age than the later teenage years.[65] Despite pressure from the authorities for head teachers to gain and maintain student numbers, they were often powerless in the face of local economic conditions that impinged upon the smooth running of centres. The key issue that had to be contended with focused on attendance. Numerous instances are cited in log books of attendance being markedly reduced for short periods due to overtime at the local factories, which was also noted by head teachers as a reason for lateness on the part of students. Economic reasons were given in a reply to comments made by the inspectors in their report of 1921 regarding the high absentee rate generally, when the head of a centre in Bermondsey noted the difficulties inherent in the area.[66] By 1921, the Bermondsey Settlement had been severely affected by unemployment and had to ask for an increase in grants from the authorities in order to run classes.[67] Another problem related to attendance occurred between late August and the end of September when poor attendance was particularly felt in the Bermondsey area during the hopping season, which saw large numbers of those living in the area decamp to the hop fields of Kent for a working holiday. Although economic factors would have been a constraint on both men and women engaging in this form of educative leisure, women may well have been less motivated than men to seek ways of continuing courses they had started. Many women may have felt that the curriculum they were offered at women's institutes often sought to reinforce their role in the domestic sphere, whereas for men, many courses on offer to them did provide them with skills to improve their employment opportunities. The education authority was often at odds with those who were providing the education service on the question of the expectations of students; one such issue was that of punctuality. Reports of inspectors noted that there were differences in the numbers recorded at classes at the first marking of registers compared to the second marking of them, and that the length of classes were longer than stated in the regulations. Explanations given by the teacher in charge often pointed to the late hours of work and poor transport with which students had to contend. Those running the classes were willing to accommodate this if young people were to be encouraged to attend classes. However, this was not always deemed acceptable on the part of the authorities. This tension between the authorities and the local providers also manifested itself in a report of a special inspection in 1933 of the Bermondsey Settlement that noted the lack of machines in the successful dressmaking class.[68] A similar lack of resources had previously been found in the typing classes and much discussion occurred between the staff and the authorities as to whether the class should be closed given the lack of adequate machines to resource the class.[69] Sometimes, the authorities' own systems worked against one another. The impact of economic conditions on the students' ability to attend classes was heightened in situations where they had to pay to attend classes. As the economic climate worsened, so potential students could not afford the fees for classes at fee-paying institutes or even the registration fee for non-fee-paying institutes. Whether an institute charged fees or not greatly affected attendance figures. This is illustrated by the case of the Fair Street Institute that was free, and had healthy attendance figures while the nearby Keetons Road, a fee-paying institute, constantly reported class closure and concerns about falling numbers.[70] Such was this an issue that the head of the institute at Keetons Road canvassed the authorities to make the institute free on the grounds of the local economic situation. Like other establishments, it noted that when fees rose, there was a corresponding fall in attendance. It is interesting to note that girls were not prepared to pay the registration fee in advance for a term even when institutes were free but would rather spend money on the cinema and dancing. This is indicative that they were actively making choices as consumers, and that what the institutes had to offer did not appeal to them.

3

The girl in the background

In 1904, Lily Montague, a co-founder of the National Organization of Girls' Clubs, contributed a chapter to a book concerning the lifestyle of boys in cities in England. The publication of the book reflected the growing anxieties about the lifestyle of youth and more so working-class youth that had intensified by the interwar period. Montague's chapter, entitled 'The Girl in the Background',[1] focused on the relationship between boys and girls, drawing attention among other things to the environmental factors that she considered had a negative influence on the lifestyle of working-class girls. In the course of explaining the lifestyle of working-class girls, she made reference to the girl only thinking about seeking pleasure and not thinking about the future. This was a theme that formed part of the concerns about working-class girls through the period. Montague did acknowledge the nature of the girl's working conditions and the quality of her home environment as reasons for the working-class girl adopting the particular lifestyle that was attributed to her. Montague's purpose was to explain the reasons for what was considered the inappropriate behaviour and attitudes of working-class girls and to suggest some strategies to encourage them to change their demeanour. 'The Girl in the Background' serves as an excellent metaphor for situating the position of girls within the contemporary discourse of the period and indeed resonated throughout much of the twentieth century. The title of Montague's chapter therefore provides a useful starting point to begin to understand why the girl has been marginalized in the analysis of the development of youthful leisure. Montague's chapter is interesting in that it clearly sets out a specific construct of who the working-class girl was expected to be and, in doing so, informed what it meant to be a girl. It was this certainty that was to shape the experience of being a girl; it was as though a template existed for her to fit into. However, the assumptions upon which the construction of this concept was based failed to acknowledge that girls were involved in the production of the world that defined them and as such they were implicated in the construction of the girl. This was to provide a challenge during the period partly because the world that defined girls was changing and, crucially for working-class girls, the concept of the modern girl was emerging and she was someone who many girls aspired to as she was proactive in asserting herself in ways that provided a space for working-class girls to become the modern girl. This draws attention to the value of considering the discourses within which the girl was constructed in the past as it will enable an understanding of what the signifiers of being a girl were and the sites at which she was defined. It has been suggested that images projected onto youth are often connected with what seems uniquely new about the period.[2] This was certainly the case during the interwar years when girls were presented with a series of paradoxes about how they should live their lives. The discursive structures through which the girl was defined, which Montague had alluded to, were based upon her role in the domestic sphere and her role in the workplace. While this construct of the girl was shared by many contemporary commentators, girls were challenging the discourses that defined the girl in the aftermath of war by drawing upon alternative constructs of the girl as they recognized that the world was changing. Soland refers to the 1910s and 1920s as a time of social and sexual upheavals which reshaped female identities and gender relations and, in doing so, sought to establish what girls would have seen as 'modern' lives for themselves.[3] Indeed, they did become highly visible during the interwar years, so much so that Soland has suggested that the 1920s were a time of transition that saw what she termed 'Victorian gender relations' across Europe fade. She argued that the young women who figured so prominently in the post-war discourse were not only the object of discourse but also central agents in the charting of new female identities.[4] This draws attention to the fact that what it means to be a girl is not static; it changes over time and is culturally specific. It has been suggested that girls 'were highly visible in twentieth-century western cultures – mostly as a marker of immature and malleable identity'.[5] Certainly, it was this perception of who the girl was that underpinned much of the debate within voluntary organizations during the interwar years as girls were not conforming to the image of who the working-class girl was expected to be. Instead, they were rejecting some constructs of the girl in favour of others and in doing so they became increasingly visible in the public domain. Their working lives, the increasing expectation of time for leisure and the expanding choice of leisure available coalesced to allow them to explore different identities that had the capacity to influence their adult identity and, in doing so, challenged constructs of who the girl should be. The shifting definitions of who the girl was unsettled ideas of who the girl should be.

The claim of Clarke et al. that youth during the latter part of the twentieth century was seen in official discourse as 'something we ought to do something about'[6] was not new. It was a theme that had resonated throughout the century to a greater or lesser degree. Since the beginning of the century, commentaries about youth and their lifestyles were invariably gender and class specific with a particular focus on issues related to working-class youth. By the interwar period, there was still some evidence in contemporary debates about youth in official discourse of the psychological theories of adolescent development made popular by G. Stanley Hall in the early years of the twentieth century.[7] Tinkler suggests that it was these ideas that informed much of the public debate about youth at that time.[8] The concept of adolescence was firmly gender- and class-differentiated in terms of how it was supposedly experienced. Gillis has argued that the term 'adolescence' was imposed on the working classes in an attempt to enhance the norms of the middle class at a time when the working classes were seen as a problem.[9] To some extent, there was evidence of this throughout the interwar years in relation to attitudes towards the leisure pursuits of teenage girls. However, rather than draw upon psychological theories of adolescent development that were still evident in contemporary debates about the lifestyle of girls during the interwar years, it is much more appropriate to perceive the girl as a social construct that is informed by the ideological tensions of contemporary understandings of class and gender relations. This will allow the nature and substance of debates about girls' leisure during the interwar years to be contextualized in relation to concerns vocalized by social investigators and other stakeholders who had a vested interest in their lifestyles. Articles in the journals of many of the voluntary organizations that provided leisure for girls reinforced assumptions made about the perceived limitations of working-class girls that, in turn, fed the image of who they assumed the girl to be. To illustrate this, a paper entitled 'The Girl of Today and Her Needs' given by Miss Forrest at the Girls' Friendly Society Conference in Wrexham stated: 'I suppose what strikes most people about the Girls' Friendly Society of today is 1. The seething restlessness and craving for excitement, leading in some cases to loose behaviour 2. Her indifference to religion and neglect of the things that matter.' Miss Forrest attributed this partly to the effects of war and indifference to religion and partly due to a lack of religious teaching both at home and at church. She also suggested that it might be the fact that occupations had changed.[10] Meanwhile, Miss Mills, a worker at the West Ham Club, said that although her girls were less rough than those at the Docklands Settlement in Bermondsey, they too lacked concentration and classes on serious subjects were not successful. They didn't like listening and no speaker could hold their attention for more than ten minutes. She said that they all thought religion meant standing aloof from their own people and forswearing amusement.[11] The tension between how club workers expected the girl to behave and how girls wanted to use their time for leisure was a constant issue throughout the period. At a conference on the subject of the religious aims of the club, Miss

Alice Hoare spoke of the problems of the girls in her club: 'loving enjoyment, liking to be in gangs ... contradictory, willful, with a desire for responsibility and to be trusted and a great faculty for hero worship'.[12] An article about character building in the Junior Club suggested that playing games encourages fairness and good manners as girls of thirteen to fifteen were inclined to be rude and what they needed was some discipline. The solution was to be found in teaching them to be reliable, to take on responsibilities, to pray and to have religious discipline.[13] It was this certainty of what was needed to ensure that girls conformed to the images that club workers had of the girl that was a source of contention. Most working-class girls had been taught from a young age that they had responsibilities within the home, they were aware of the need for discipline in the workplace and of the consequences of not conforming to the rules. What many of the club workers wanted was for girls to conform to their image of who the working-class girl should be.

The wide range of different organizations represented at the National Conference on the Leisure of the People in 1919[14] reveals the high level of interest in the lifestyles of young people across the social spectrum. Equally, the themes of the discussions at this conference reflected the eclectic array of social and cultural aspects of the lives of youth generally that were deemed to be considered aspects of leisure. What was prescient was the underlying recognition that the environment was to a great extent the key to the problems aired about the use of leisure. Certainly, this was the case in terms of the development of the working-class girl; it was acknowledged by social commentators and underpinned many of the debates concerning the ways that the girl was constructed during the period. Burns, for example, writing in 1932, reinforced the idea that the environment was crucial in the development of young people, suggesting that adolescence involved particular problems in the modern world that were attributed to the rapid social and industrial changes.[15] In relation to girls specifically, Soland has argued that the obsession with women's roles and behaviour reflected a more general anxiety over social disorder, socio-economic change and the collapse of long-standing moral and ideological doctrines in the post-war period.[16] This was clearly evident in the debates that took place within the organizations that provided leisure for girls, such as the Girls' Friendly Society and the National Organization of Girls' Clubs. An article entitled 'Women's Position after the War' in *the Girls' Club Journal* in 1918 talked of the way that women's lives had been changed by war in terms of greater job opportunities and a wider range of jobs available. The author recognized that 'in the post-war period women will be back in the home as the jobs will have to be filled by men'.[17] In the same journal, another article confirmed that in the post-war period leisure would be seen as more important. In recognition of there being greater time for leisure, the author talked of the need to focus more sharply on what leisure should consist of.[18]

During the interwar period, the concerns about working-class girls fed into the ongoing theme of instability in the modern world that Soland made reference to. They were seen as vulnerable as they were often considered ill-advised by their families and, according to some, entered the world of work at what was considered an early age.[19] The upheavals of the war, including the dislocation of the family, and the changing society post-war were all seen as indicators of the need to support working-class girls in order to remedy what was thought to be lacking in their lives. Implicit in this perception was a clear statement about how the girl should conduct herself. An article appeared in the *Daily Mail* in 1920 attempting to persuade women to volunteer as workers in girls' clubs, especially in London. The article is interesting in that it firmly establishes the idea that the girls' club would refine the working-class girl in some way. In trying to explain the nature of the work involved, the author described the club thus: 'The girls' club is to the working-girl what a finishing school is to her better-off sister, and she is anxious to learn things that will help her either with her trade or with her home if she marries.'[20] As the period progressed, girls were also seen as needing guidance in relation to becoming good citizens, particularly so when women became entitled to vote.

A powerful framework within which the girl was constructed was the discourse of domesticity. The ideological location of women in the domestic sphere was firmly entrenched across the social classes. Becoming wives and mothers was perceived to be their destiny. Montague talked of the ways in which many working-class girls could be of value in their role of being a wife, but due to environmental factors they often had limited training and did not consider the longer-term implications of their actions.[21] How this role was taken on was very clearly class specific. For upper-class girls and some middle-class girls their future role would be to run the household via servants, while working-class girls knew they would have to manage a very different sort of home: caring for children, managing the household and quite likely engaging in paid work either within the home or outside of it. The ideology of a woman's place being within the home had been, as Beddoe has noted, firmly re-established in the immediate aftermath of the war.[22] During the early post-war period, there had been a rigorous campaign encouraging women back into the domestic sphere after they had visibly entered into the world of work outside of the home on a full-time basis during the First World War. The result was, as Beddoe has shown, that by 1921 the female participation rate in the workforce was 2 per cent lower than it had been in 1911.[23] While such figures reinforce the point that the ideological place for women was in the home, they do not necessarily include all women who worked, as those who were employed in casual or non-insured occupations were not always included in statistics. The preordained role of the girl in the domestic sphere was reinforced in the careers advice offered to girls. A booklet aimed at the parents of those of school-leaving age persuaded them that dressmaking, ladies tailoring and millinery trades offered something good for the average type of girl who was leaving school. The booklet made the point that these trades were not blind alley work: 'The girl learns a trade, which is useful to her … and when she has a home of her own later on in life, she will be able to make the bulk – if not all – of her own and her children's clothes, and also neatly repair her husband's attire.'[24] The ability on the part of the working-class girl to take on her 'natural' role in the domestic sphere as wife and mother was seen as an issue throughout the period. Her supposed deficiency in being able to manage the household was often based upon somewhat tenuous evidence arising from assumptions about her lifestyle. In reality, the evidence bore little resemblance to the girl's role within the domestic sphere; the presumptions made about her demonstrated a lack of awareness of the realities of working-class life on the part of some social commentators. However, this was not always the case. Many of those who worked with girls were acutely aware of the quality of the environment that the girls lived in and sought to provide them with the means to ensure that they could have a better life in the future. The irony is that, from an early age, girls were inculcated into their ideological position in the domestic sphere that was clearly gendered in that it was the accepted norm that they took on many of the household chores. The gendered nature of who completed chores in the home was observed by Mess: 'The heavy task is taken over by the daughters; while … the boys are usually allowed to play, the girls must assist in running the home, looking after children, going on errands, any of the multitudinous jobs that must be done.'[25] Grace Tarbuck, who grew up in Lambeth during the interwar years, recalled: 'They've [the boys] got it easy. The girls had to do it all. Had to make the beds, sweep the rooms out, scrub the floors, shake the carpet.'[26] Her experience would have resonated with working-class girls around the country. Even when working-class girls left school and started work, their role within the family continued to be one of supporting their mothers. They were still expected to take on chores within the home, unlike their brothers who were likely absolved of any work within the home. Mary recalls when she had found herself a job, 'On a Saturday morning there'd be go out there and wash them chairs for me and put some carbolic in the water make it all nice and white. We all had our jobs to do and we all got on with it after a little moan and groan.'[27] Often, the burden of helping their mothers fell on the eldest daughter. Maude noted: 'I had two brothers and seven sisters. I was the eldest one of the lot which was very painful at times, I used to have to take them all in the park, being the eldest.'[28] The working-class girl was in essence an apprentice, training to take on the role of wife and mother – but in a working-class household. Significantly, some social commentators who expressed concerns about girls' ability to take on managing the household often failed to take this into account and instead continued to try to persuade teenage girls to attend cooking, sewing and housewifery classes in the evenings. The lack of understanding of the reality of working-class girls' lives was reflected in a Ministry of Reconstruction report in 1919 that focused on the pressing issue of the day, namely the lack of girls wishing to go into domestic service. It was suggested that the lack of training for domestic work lay at the root of the problem. In order to entice girls into domestic service, the suggested solution was for more facilities to train girls in domestic work for two years after they left school. It was pointed out that housework should be seen as their 'natural vocation'.[29] This was a theme that was to resonate throughout the period as girls were making their own decisions about the nature of the employment that they wished to take up. The author of the report clearly had little understanding of the fact that as soon as girls left school they entered the world of work where they spent long hours working outside of the home and they often had chores to attend to when they arrived home. It is unlikely that they would voluntarily attend evening classes to improve their skills in domestic chores. When Miss Massey, the responsible mistress at the New Park Road Evening Institute, wrote to the manager of the Royal Arsenal Co-Operative Bakery at Brixton Hill asking if she could visit the bakery to talk to girls about the classes on offer at the New Park Road Evening Institute, the bakery manager Mr Williams complied with her request, suggesting a suitable time for her visit. Her aim was to encourage girls to attend evening classes where they could learn cookery skills, how to clean a house and sewing. A copy of the letter she sent to Mr Williams in her own handwriting records the outcome of her visit. It reads: 'Result of Interview: Stoic Indifference – nobody came – Type – rather rough class of woman.'[30] Oral testimony suggests that teenage girls accepted that they had to help their mothers despite having worked long hours during the day. Frequently, they felt a sense of responsibility to support their mothers out of an awareness of the drudgery of their daily lives. When women who had grown up during the period reflect upon their youthful lives, they often refer to their mothers as 'poor things' who had hard lives. Jessie Stephen, a local councillor in Bermondsey during the interwar years, described the life of an average Bermondsey woman:

Just a drab, dreary round of housework and trying to make one penny do the work of two. ... Frequently she is compelled in order to supplement the family income to go to work in a factory. In that case her work has to be done in the evenings or before she sets off for the factory in the mornings.[31]

The idea that girls might have a better quality of life than their mothers was not lost on some of the workers in the Girls' Club movement. An article entitled

'Amusement and its Place in Religious Life' suggested 'It is probably true to say that many girls snatch at pleasure because, looking at their mothers, they think they are not likely to have any more amusement when they get older.'[32] This was likely to be true. Although those working in clubs were vocal in their concerns about the ways in which some girls chose to spend their leisure time, many club workers were aware of the reasons for girls behaving in ways that they disapproved of. For example, club workers often commented on the boisterous behaviour of girls; nevertheless, they would also qualify their concerns by pointing out that girls needed to let off steam having been employed in a factory all day, or it was due to simply having some space that they did not have in their home. However, for some club workers it indicated a lack of restraint on the part of girls and it was felt that they needed to be trained to be more ladylike.

As the interwar years progressed, girls came to realize that they could expect a lifestyle somewhat different to their mothers and this included their future role in the domestic sphere.[33] The decline in family size that was especially evident among working-class families throughout the period[34] relieved girls of having to care for younger siblings. The growing provision of welfare facilities such as maternity clinics and child welfare clinics, and the generally improved medical facilities for women in areas of the country such as Bermondsey, meant that fewer girls were likely to have to take on the responsibility of running the household if their mother became ill and this made a qualitative difference to their lives. As well as benefiting from improved welfare facilities, girls in Bermondsey were better off than some girls in different parts of the country in other ways. A responsibility that often fell on girls was dealing with the family washing. Mrs Mitchell, who grew up in Lancashire, recalled the arduous task of doing the washing in the boiler in the back kitchen,[35] whereas girls living in areas such as Bermondsey, where new state-of-the-art wash houses had been installed by 1925, would have been relieved of the burden of the hard work that Mrs Mitchell had to endure as they could just put the washing in machines and then collect it later. It was relatively simple things like this that provided girls with significant changes in the nature of their lives that gave them more freedom. Despite this, the discourse of domesticity firmly set out the future for girls as wives and mothers and in doing so had an impact on their working lives. The idea that the working lives of girls was a temporary role until they married was perpetuated by organizations like the Pilgrim Trust which reinforced images of women's lives being dominated by the idea of marriage and family: 'The girl of fourteen tends to drift into the most remunerative employment immediately available, keeping the alternative of marriage always in view and hoping that she will sooner or later be freed from the fulfilment of a function in industry.'[36] This view did not reflect the reality of their lives. Most working-class girls left school at the age of fourteen. They recall very vividly leaving school on the Friday and starting work on the Monday; they were aware that 'it was a case of having to'. The urgency for them to have a job was because their wages were crucial in the family struggle against poverty. In 1921, leaving school aged fourteen, Mary spent a week at home without having found employment. This was quite unusual for girls, so much so that her mother promptly took her to a local factory and got her a job. For Sarah, there was little choice of what work she did. 'I was a nice needle worker. I wanted to go and be a dressmaker. ... I wanted to be apprenticed, but it wasn't much money, 'cos I was the first one born so I had to go to work.' Lily recalled her first job: 'I left school at fourteen, I always wanted to be a dressmaker instead I went to Cooper Dennison and Waltons first of all I used to have to do the labels you know the labels they put on all the luggage, then they moved me up into the stock room and I went on the eyelet machine, when I first went there I earned eight shillings a week.'[37] On the whole, girls were fatalistic about acknowledging what was needed in order for the family to survive. A publication entitled *A Guide to the Employment for London Boys and Girls*, published in 1928, noted that only one in seven boys and girls were still at school at the age of fifteen.[38] This small number across London was mirrored in Bermondsey where the majority of young people left school at the age of fourteen. Such was this the norm that, when the authorities proposed that young people should stay at school until the end of the term in which they were fourteen, the issue was raised as an item for discussion by the Bermondsey Borough Council Education Committee.[39] Here, it was argued that the proposal was unjust as many young people often had a job lined up ready to start that would then be lost. The LCC, which had responsibility for education across London, was asked to adjust the ruling so that young people could leave school if they found suitable employment. Girls would have felt the pressure to leave school at the earliest age possible as factory jobs expanded during the interwar years. For many girls, the nature of the work was irrelevant: 'It didn't matter to me what I did you had to go to work in them days otherwise there was nothing for you.'[40] Work increasingly came to shape girls' lives. Referring to the interwar period, Elizabeth Roberts has pointed out that the period between leaving school and taking up the role of wife and mother was distinctive as more girls and young women between the ages of fourteen and twenty-five worked for wages during this period than at any other time in their lives.[41]

The stark change from being a schoolgirl to being a young worker was without any rite of passage. Rose echoed the memories of many women concerning the lack of transition between childhood and adulthood and the ways in which life changed overnight when she said 'it was abrupt and final'.[42] While there was a lack of transition from childhood to being a young worker, girls were still expected to take on chores within the home when they started work, but some restraints were lifted. For many working-class girls, the period between leaving school and setting up their own home did hold some freedom that their mothers had lacked. The social independence, which both Langhamer and Davies noticed, that was given to young wage earners reflected the value of these relatively affluent wage earners to the family.[43] It was common practice in households around the country for girls to give up their wages each week to their mother. Girls were given back some 'spends' from their mother; the amount they received in return varied, as did what they were expected to use the money for. Both Glucksmann and Jerry White have drawn attention to the fact that the labour market at this time was structured by age, region and marital status.[44] What is interesting is that this did not always work to the detriment of teenage girls, and evidence demonstrating otherwise will be shown. Working-class girls had always worked outside of the home, but what changed during the interwar years was the nature of the work that many girls were engaged in. Glucksmann has documented how women were at the forefront of the growing light industries, particularly in the Midlands and the south of England during this period, arguing that they 'assumed a new and heightened significance' as workers.[45] Notably, it was girls rather than older married women who were in fact in demand in these industries; certainly, there is clear evidence of this in Bermondsey. Nearly half of the total number of women working in the jam, sugar and confectionery trades, all of which adopted many of the new production processes, were below the age of twenty.[46] For girls growing up in the area, mechanization of the production process in a number of industries worked to their advantage in terms of gaining employment. An example was biscuit production, where 70 per cent of operatives were women, of whom 23 per cent were under eighteen.[47] This was particularly significant in London where 40 per cent of biscuit manufacturing took place; more specifically, Peek Frean, which was located in Bermondsey, was one of the major companies producing biscuits.[48] It was a company that introduced mechanized production processes very early during the interwar years and as a consequence the composition of the workforce changed to the advantage of girls. These changes in the production process meant that there was a reduced demand for skilled workers and, as a result, fewer men were required for the diminishing number of skilled jobs. At the same time, the demand for unskilled workers increased, thereby creating opportunities for women workers and more specifically teenage girls for the routine semi-skilled or unskilled tasks that the new production processes required. As the company operated a strict marriage bar, this increased the demand for teenage girls to take up employment at the factory as women had to leave once they married. It meant that teenage girls were confident of finding work in an economic climate where the priority was to remain in some form of employment, irrespective of the nature of the

FIGURE 1 *Making toys at a factory. Courtesy of Mary Evans Picture Library.*

work. Changes in the production processes in two other industries that were dominant in Bermondsey also affected girls' employment opportunities in a positive way. The use of mechanical processes in the metal box industry meant that the work was seen to be particularly suitable for women and girls; as a consequence, this stimulated a greater demand for female employees. In fact, in the metal trades in 1891, the proportion of female labour had been hardly more than one in fifty, yet by 1929 it was more than one in five.[49] While many girls living in Bermondsey felt the impact of the modern production processes to be found in factories in the area, there were others who worked in smaller workshops and as a consequence experienced a very different working life. What these girls had in common is that invariably they were poorly paid for the work that they did. Dressmaking was another area of work that employed large numbers of women. The processes in this industry became simplified during the interwar period due to the changing styles of dress which led to the development of mass production techniques requiring a less-skilled workforce. As with other industries that had modernized their production process, once the work process was deskilled it meant that there was a greater demand for women workers in factories; in fact, nine out of ten workers in this industry were women.[50] Another significant feature of this industry was that the majority of workers in this sector were on piece work rates of pay: those who started at the age of fourteen as runners might earn the piece work minimum of 8d. per hour, while girls who worked on simple processes earned between 9s. 10d. and 11s. per week.[51] The nature of the work available had a serious impact on the quality of girls' lives. While concern was expressed about the practice of piece work rates of pay in factories employing many teenage girls, such concerns were not always shared by the girls themselves. For them, piece work meant that they were able to have some control through the speed with which they worked and thereby the amount of money they earned. For example, Alice talking of her first job as a machinist recalled: 'You didn't earn a lot of money … two shillings and six-pence a week for a year and the second year I got two shillings and six-pence rise to five shillings and then when you're sixteen then you go piece work and then you earn what you do don't you?' Once Alice reached this age, she was in control of what she could earn.

Because of the seasonal and casual nature of much of the factory work available to girls and women in this trade, it is often difficult to gather precise information about fluctuations in rates of pay. However, it would be wrong to assume that the earning capacity of women and girls was particularly high; what was more to the point was that it was regular. Manufacturing and food processing, which were two of the dominant industries in the area, also preferred female labour because as many commentators noted, women did not mind the monotony of such work. When Priestley visited a factory in Leicester, the manager told him that, in his experience,

> girls preferred purely routine and monotonous jobs because once they had learned the fairly simple necessary movements they could then work all day and think about something else while they were working. Their fingers would be busy with the sewing machines or irons, but their minds could be far away, wondering how Elsie was getting on with Joe or brooding over the film stars male and female.[52]

The preference for employing young girls in factories was reaffirmed by Jephcott almost a decade later when she observed what she considered the reasons for their employment. 'There is always a large demand for young girls for factory work because girls of 14 and 15 have good eyesight, quick fingers and quick wits; they have no experience to sell and their financial responsibilities at home are not so heavy as those of older people.'[53] She also suggested that, from an employer's point of view, 'girls are less impatient of monotonous work than boys'. She quoted an employment exchange official stating: 'they just sit around the bench and move their fingers and talk about their boys. It's like knitting for them.'[54] Rooff confirmed this, noting that where new machinery was introduced there was a tendency for girls to be kept on rather than boys or adults as girls took more kindly to repetitive processes.[55] Durant was not so positive about the repetitive nature of the production process. Commenting upon the nature of the work that many girls were engaged in, he stated, 'Their jobs are suitable for "headless" people.' He continued, 'The girls become stupefied with the boredom their work requires.'[56] The notion that girls might experience job satisfaction is interesting as it raises the question of whether anyone asked girls what they thought about their role in the workplace. When Harley carried out a study of attitudes to work and the leisure pursuits of young girls in Manchester, she noted that the girls who were employed in a range of different jobs found their work interesting for a variety of reasons; of most significance was the camaraderie that they welcomed.[57] Certainly, for many girls, working on the production line allowed them to develop this camaraderie. Jephcott was interested in finding out what made dull jobs bearable to girls. Her research revealed that girls made sense of their working lives partly by acknowledging what it enabled them to do outside of the workplace; work was seen as instrumental. While Jephcott expressed surprise that girls prioritized talking about their leisure rather than work,[58] their emphasis on talking about their leisure pursuits is understandable as girls had very little choice in the type of work they took up, but they did have a choice of what leisure to pursue. Despite being prominent in the modern production process, it did not mean that girls necessarily took their consciousness from this. As Yeo has suggested, the consciousness of individuals occurred outside the workplace.[59] This was especially so for teenage girls who sought their consciousness through their participation in leisure rather than work. Girls growing up during this period had a realistic view of what the working world was like in terms of pay and conditions and they knew that their priority was to ensure that they could contribute to the family income. Holtby commented: 'Young girls are working in factories, private domestic work, shops and laundries, and using the small wage to support their parents.'[60] The ability to work was also important as it meant that girls gained some semblance of independence in terms of the 'spends' they received which they could use as they wished.[61] Age clearly became an important determinant when gaining employment and girls working in areas of the country where new industries were flourishing were in demand as workers.[62] Holtby acknowledged that young working-class girls became distinguished from their parents and siblings through their workplace culture, and their leisure and mobility between jobs. She noted, 'As it is often easier for women than for men to find employment, so it is easier for adolescents than for adults.'[63] This would have been the case in areas like Bermondsey, and it would have had an impact, subtle or otherwise, on relationships between family members; for girls it would have boosted their confidence in terms of their ability to find work.

Although it was also acknowledged by girls that when they married they might be likely to take on the sort of work that their mothers did as charwomen or take in washing, they were, however, aware that their world was changing and that there was the possibility for a different sort of life in the future. Girls living in areas where it was relatively easy to gain some form of employment may have felt a sense of empowerment but they were acutely aware of the ways in which employers made use of them until they might have to pay them an adult wage: 'It wasn't difficult to find work if you were very young, because people used to take you on till you were eighteen and you wanted higher wages and then you got the sack and they took on the next group of youngsters to do the job.'[64] While social investigators lobbied government agencies about the levels of pay that girls received for the hours they worked and the processes that some employers used to ensure that they did not have to pay girls an adult wage, girls themselves were not concerned about long-term job security. They knew that they could get another job easily, albeit of a similar nature. The demand for unskilled labour was confirmed in comments made by Miss Knight, a representative from the Tower Bridge Evening Institute. Speaking at a conference on Juvenile Delinquency, she noted the problem of a shortage of what she interestingly termed 'child labour', that is, unskilled workers aged fourteen to sixteen.[65] The seasonal nature of the work in some industries meant that girls needed to be mobile and to be prepared to go from one job to another. In the clothing trade, girls were often taken on as learners during the busy season, paid a few shillings a week and then dismissed. Because of the competition for jobs that were considered respectable, employers could 'train' girls for up to three years on processes that only took six months to learn, paying them small wages.[66] Pay was an issue for women generally. They had to be flexible in terms of accepting different methods of being paid; despite doing the same job as a man, they would often be paid a woman's rate. Women and girls were more likely than men to be paid a piece rate than time rate for work and they found their rates of pay were lowered if they earned too much. In the tailoring trade, outworkers were often paid less than indoor hands for the same task. The *Bermondsey Labour Magazine* reported in September 1921 that in the dressmaking trade there was a drastic reduction in rates of pay for young girls of fourteen years of age learning the retail bespoke branch of the trade. Their rate of pay was reduced from 2s. 4 ½d. to 1s. ½d.[67] The amount of pay that girls received was crucial and often determined whether they stayed in a job or not. Lizzie, who gained employment at a tailors, recalled, 'I didn't really like it and it was only eight shillings and six-pence a week so eventually I tried the Alaska [fur] factory and I got paid more there, you first went there at fourteen, you got twenty-five shillings which was more than any other factory.' As the period progressed, a wider range of occupations became available to young girls; however, as writers such as Jerry White have indicated, the extent that such opportunities were taken up was often limited.[68] Although teenage girls might see the potential of a greater array of job opportunities available to them, the reality of their lives was such that invariably they took on whatever work was available in the locality, for, as McKibbin has noted, the English labour market was still largely based upon local economies.[69] It was this crucial feature that had an impact on teenage girls becoming consumers as well as producers. This would have been partly due to the practicalities of having to pay for travel and the time taken up travelling and partly due to the traditional cultural practices of how individuals gained a job. The diversity of employment for girls in London generally, and more specifically in Bermondsey, meant that they could gain work with relative ease. Mary recalled: 'You could go out of one job and into another then, I mean if you didn't like it you could leave it.' There was, however, a shift during the period from gaining a job locally by word of mouth and family contacts to girls being able to gain employment further afield in London with the growth of retail and light industry and clerical posts as the period progressed. While this provided girls with a confidence that they could find work, it was their ability to move from job to job that concerned many politicians and social investigators, who saw this as feckless, and as Todd has pointed out it did not fit with the idea of what the social investigators termed 'self-improvement'.[70] Indeed, Miss Knight made the observation that in her district of Tower Bridge Road in Bermondsey, girls were very independent and moved from job to job.[71] It does reveal a gulf in understanding their motivation; for girls it was a way of improving their choices and often improving the money they earned. Both Fowler[72] and McKibbin[73] suggest that by the 1920s, the main appeal of work for young people was the opportunity to gain some spending money. Certainly, the potential to gain employment had clear ramifications for their capacity to engage with the new leisure activities that became available during the interwar years. But, for many young people, they had no choice: they were acutely aware from a young age of their family's economic circumstances and the need for them to contribute to the family budget. For the working classes, the neighbourhood could be a valuable resource in numerous ways. One aspect was the sharing of information about job opportunities, which was not new. Writing in the late nineteenth century about young girls going into factory work, Frances Hicks had noticed: 'A neighbour or a "mate" … tells them that the foreman is taking on hands at a certain factory and they go and take their chance at the factory gates. It does not matter in the least that they know nothing of the work.'[74] This was still the case by the interwar years, as Sarah, who was born in 1914, recalled:

I had lots of jobs. I worked in the sausage factory down Spa Road, twisting the skins. It wasn't easy you know at first. A friend of mine up the road said to me 'Do you want a job?' I said 'Yeah.' She said 'Can you twist skins?' I said no I couldn't, so she said 'come on I'll show you', and took me round the factory and I had a go.

Monitoring of the working lives of young people increased during this period with investigations being carried out in different parts of the country focusing on a range of issues including how young people acquired their first job and the nature of the juvenile labour market.[75] Many girls starting their working lives during this period got jobs by word of mouth.[76] Alice recalled getting her first job: 'Someone down the road got it for me she worked there.'[77]

Glucksmann has argued that at the time, women were not only part of the production process, but they also became consumers of the goods they were producing.[78] A good example of this was noted in an article entitled 'Thanks to Fashion Fad,' which pointed out, 'Because of the latest fad for wearing ankle socks – a section of the hosiery industry at Nottingham is working overtime to cope with the demand.' It was reported that, at one factory, male workers were earning up to £7 per week, while girls were making up to £3 per week. Despite the girls earning less than the male workers, they were nevertheless benefiting financially from the demand for ankle socks.[79]

For girls who dominated the assembly lines, this positioning not only provided them with an assurance that they could find work, but it would have also provided them with a realization that the changing nature of work would have an impact on other areas of their lives including their leisure pursuits. Those working in the dressmaking and tailoring trades were able to see the latest fashions, and girls working on the production line were often able to share ideas about their leisure pursuits. Alice, who started work training to be a tailor, recalled what she spent her money on once she started work: 'More luxuries, clothes, when you work amongst new styles you want it don't you? You want new styles, time you bought the material and the shoes I mean to buy the best pair of shoes it was only twelve shillings and sixpence. Used to go down the Blue to Steeles 'cos that was a real high class shop then.' It became common practice for girls to make instrumental use of the workplace to gain access to what they considered leisure to be.

A key issue that personified girls asserting themselves in the world of work and creating identities of their choosing during the period was that of the servant problem. In the aftermath of the First World War, there was a decline in the numbers of girls wishing to enter domestic service. Instead, they were looking for work elsewhere, so much so that 'the servant problem' became a prominent issue in the context of more general debates concerning the lifestyle of working-class girls. The lack of popularity of going into domestic service caused great consternation throughout the period. For many commentators, it linked in with concerns about stability in the context of girls' rightful place being in the domestic sphere and, as a consequence, service was seen to be the most 'natural attribute' for the girl. In areas of the country where having left school, girls would have traditionally gone into domestic service, the war had provided them with possibilities for alternative forms of work which girls found much more attractive; shop work and even factory work potentially gave them a better quality of working life. It meant that they were not beholden to their employers' every whim; they would have had the possibility of more freedom and a greater degree of sociability at work. For girls, the factory was better than domestic service; it was often freer, they had company and some factories had social clubs attached to the workplace. As Robert Roberts noted, girls would try their hand at any job rather than domestic service.[80] The refusal to enter domestic service on their part illustrates how the discourses of domesticity and work intersected and were challenged by girls who were demonstrating that they were part of the world that constructed them but they also knew that they could challenge assumptions of who they should be and as such they felt that they could challenge the assumptions made about who they should be.

The choices that girls were making often confronted long-standing assumptions about their role in the working world. Many organizations that worked with teenage girls concerned themselves with developing strategies to make going into service more appealing to girls and to convince them that it would be a beneficial experience. For example, the Girls' Friendly Society had, since its foundation, focused on the welfare and moral education of servants. Realizing that something needed to be done to attract more girls into domestic service, an agreement was reached at a conference in 1921 that training and qualifications would raise the status of domestic service, which resulted in the setting up of the League of Skilled Housecraft to provide training to achieve this. Unfortunately, it was not qualifications that girls wanted, but freedom to have time for leisure like those who were in other forms of employment. It was precisely because of the time constraints put upon servants that many girls no longer wished to go into domestic service. As the period progressed and the nature of the work for girls expanded, the girl became defined to some extent in relation to the type of work she did, with jobs being accorded a hierarchy of status. There were perceived to be differences between the shop girl, the factory girl and the servant, each label imbued with meaning that signified social status. The lack of status of domestic service became very clear to young girls when a member of the Girls' Friendly Society wrote a letter to the editor of its magazine requesting a discussion page connected with branch news; the first topic suggested was 'Why do shop and office girls hold domestic servants in contempt?' The writer (a servant) spoke of how girls held servants in contempt; she stated, 'Possibly it is the fact that shop girls wear their hair in a "pig tail" longer than is possible for servants, follow the latest fashions more devotedly, feel more inclined to smoke cigarettes .... I admit that as a rule those girls have greater knowledge of modern accomplishments – such as shorthand, typewriting, music and dancing.'[81] The servant girl who wrote the letter summed up aptly the perceived images of these different aspects of girls' working lives. However, by 1931, Llewellyn-Smith was able to bolster the image of the servant, observing that 'with the better pay that she now commands the domestic servant is quite as well dressed as others in her class'.[82] Of course, what he was affirming was the continued emphasis that persisted throughout the period of the importance of style defining the individual. This was something that did not elude most working-class girls. An article in the *Girls' Club Journal* that attempted to provide a positive image of domestic service as a career noted: 'We are all aware of the prejudice, prevalent amongst girls to-day, against domestic service as a career.' The writer went on to persuade the reader of the appeal of going into service:

> There is more opportunity in domestic service for an odd half hour, which can, if the girl is so disposed, be devoted to reading. The factory or shop girl has no such opportunities, and her evenings are invariably spent with friends or in places of amusement – principally the latter, because the prevalence of cinemas has made the home life of the ordinary working girl almost non-existent. … As girls in service do not go out every evening attending dancing halls, etc, there is not so much temptation to spend money and to compete in clothes.[83]

For many girls, it was true that home life was almost non-existent but this was due to their cramped living conditions rather than the advent of the cinema luring them away from home. Not all girls rejected domestic service as a form of employment; some girls were attracted to the idea of going into service. Iris recalled having had lots of factory jobs when she first left school before she went into service:

> I chose to go 'cos the woman next door she was in service and she asked me if I'd like to go and that's how I got into it. I got up to cook. I got used to it and I liked it with a day off a week, I think I was 19 when I went in. I wasn't a cook straight away, you had to do the cleaning, washing all the dishes and all the rest of it and you gradually learnt. I was Marble Arch way it was a different life altogether, I was at Royal Mews, I was kitchen maid there first and I was cook for the Equerry.[84]

Girls were clearly involved in the production of the world that defined them. They were making choices where possible about the nature of the work they took up. They were also increasingly aware as the period progressed that they had an entitlement to leisure and, more importantly, they had greater choices in terms of the type of leisure available to them. The 'modern' girl was asserting herself not only in terms of her position in the workplace but also in terms of how she used her leisure time, much of which would have focused on perfecting the image of the 'modern' girl. At the beginning of the interwar years, the broad spectrum of girls' clubs generally assumed that girls needed guidance in becoming wives and mothers, but what evolved as the period progressed was an awareness that girls were growing up in a changing world and while their destiny was to be wives and mothers, they might well need a different sort of guidance. This growing awareness of a changing world was reflected in the ongoing debates to be found in the journals of the various organizations providing clubs for girls. Their articles provide ample evidence of the tensions between the narratives of who the working-class girl should be and the construct of the girl that working-class girls were choosing to be. Ironically, what increasingly became an issue for club workers was how to deal with the fact that working-class girls were asserting themselves and making their own choices about how to spend their leisure time in ways that did not always accord with what club workers thought they should be doing. Those working in the Girls' Club movement often perceived this as part of the new world and a problem of the modern age. However, the idea that working-class girls were asserting themselves was not new. They had long determined how they wished to behave, but what was different by the interwar years was that they had more choices and a greater amount of time for leisure. The fact that voluntary organizations felt the need to reappraise what they had to offer girls does suggest that the assertiveness on the part of girls in determining how to spend their leisure time was working. It also reveals how some club workers did not understand why working-class girls might prefer the pursuits that the commercial leisure sector had to offer them rather than the activities that the club might provide. The journals of many of the girls' clubs provide evidence of the lack of understanding on the part of some of those working in the Girls' Club movement about how girls used their time for leisure. Often, club workers categorized different types of girls and this was used as a basis for assumptions about how they used their time for leisure. An article entitled 'The Mind of the Girl' set out to describe the different types of girl; the author noted:

> Another kind of girl is often found among young factory workers – the girl who takes an interest in nothing at all. She doesn't want to knit, she can't sing, she is too tired to join in games or drill, and if she does condescend to dance languidly for a few minutes, she will soon drop into the easiest chair she can find and gaze listlessly in front of her.[85]

The author looked to the possibility of a monotonous job causing this attitude.

Ironically, the frivolity that many girls exhibited was indeed a reaction against the nature of their work. Similarly, another article in a journal entitled *Girls' Clubs and Politics* referred to the characteristics of members based upon

FIGURE 2 *Girls striding out. Courtesy of Jean Holder.*

the nature of their employment. Clubs with a membership which was almost exclusively factory hands and laundry workers, for example, were seen as normally good-hearted generous girls who were loyal, but apt to be governed by emotion, very easily influenced and didn't stop to question things. Such girls, it was suggested, were usually shut up in a factory or workshop all day being told what to do. When they came to the club, they wanted to let off steam. The desire for self-display was very noticeable as they were noisy and loud in order to get attention. The writer noted that the girl's own feelings formed a large part of her outlook on life and the club leader had a job to teach her self-government, let alone the principles of politics. Conversation was often about boys; politics was a lot less interesting. Another type of club girl described was the business clerk, cashier or shop assistant. She was considered a little better educated and having more chance of meeting educated people as part of her work. But once she started work, she became full of herself and her own importance and resented advice.[86] Implicit in these descriptions is a series of assumptions that drew attention to the supposed deficiencies that working-class girls exhibited in that they did not conform to the model of the working-class girl that the club worker wanted her to be. While there is some recognition of the arduous nature of the girl's working life, it did not deter negative judgements being made about the girl who was resisting becoming the model of the girl that the club workers wanted her to be. The disparity between who the girl was perceived to be during the interwar years and how she has been understood by those mapping the development of youth culture reinforces the idea that all aspects of identity are fluid and that categories of identity are not fixed but are particular to a specific moment in time. As such, concepts such as 'the girl' are unstable as they have different meanings according to the context in which they are being discussed. In the same way, conceptualizing class is specific to a particular historical moment. What becomes evident throughout the period is that girls were making choices about their use of their freedom from work as time for leisure increased. The subtle changes that slowly improved the lives of many girls in the domestic sphere and the demand for their labour in the workplace did not mean that they could suddenly experience the quality of life that those in the middle classes had, but it did mean that they were far from being in the background. Instead, they were emerging to take on the mantle of the modern girl, which was personified no more so than in their use of leisure.

4

The modern girl: Spoilt for choice

Delivering a lecture at the Institute of Hygiene in London in 1920, Dr R. Murray Leslie talked of the freedom of the modern independent girl from the supervision of her parents, the tendency to rebel against discipline, the cry of pleasure for pleasure's sake. He suggested that this encouraged a lower standard of morality. Referring to the different types of women emerging post war, he made reference to 'the social butterfly type' and described her as 'frivolous, scantily clad, jazzing flapper, irresponsible and undisciplined, to whom a new dance, a new hat, or a man with a car were of more importance than the fate of nations'.[1] The image he portrayed of the modern girl was one that became familiar and the concerns he expressed resonated throughout the period. Her leisure pursuits received a great deal of attention from an array of different groups who felt that they had a claim on her identity as she became more visible in public spaces. The growing visibility of the girl did, to some extent, act as a barometer of cultural changes and continuities. Her behaviour sparked considerable debate in the press. A letter to the *Yorkshire Post and Leeds Intelligencer* entitled 'Modern Women' was a response to a previous letter that had been published in the newspaper. The author asked whether bishops and ladies had forgotten the days of their youth. She went on to talk of the way that, during the Victorian period, people were appalled at the behaviour of young girls. She stated, 'The girl had always been the source of concern,' pointing out that the modern girl in her youth was every bit as shocking as the girl of 1921:

> The girl of today, as a rule, is much more practical, much more capable, perhaps less sentimental … than her grandmother and if she is a bit more slangy and less ladylike … think of what her environment has been during

the last few years? Not the sheltered cloister of a puritanical home, but the munitions factory, the Field hospital, the Shell strewn Road, in a motor car.[2]

The letter was signed *A mother of three modern girls*. The author of this letter was correct that concerns about the girl were not new, but what was distinctive by the interwar period was the focus on the nature of girls' leisure. The mother was firmly linking the behaviour and attitudes of girls to their experiences during the war. The discursive framework within which the girl was defined was changing in ways that provided her with the potential to be involved in defining who she wanted to be. What was becoming apparent was the growing independence of the young girl, which was reflected in her assertiveness in choosing how she spent her leisure time and the public persona she created, and in doing so she was shaping who she wanted to be rather than who others wanted her to be. The resolve of girls to determine how they used their leisure time became the subject of consternation, often causing strong reaction to the choices they made. At the 28th Annual Meeting of the Ladies Home Mission Union of the Church Pastoral Aid Society, the Chair spoke of how 'the lure of pleasure and the love of amusement had so caught the girls of the country that practically their mental balance was unhinged and lost'.[3] There were others who had a very different opinion about what the lifestyle of modern girls told society. On her retirement as superintendent of the Northampton Polytechnic Institute, Miss Alice M. Tuck expressed her view of the modern girl: 'She is more sensible than girls were when I joined this Institute. She makes a better companion, and I find it easier to get on with her. As for their short skirts I think they are very nice, and as well as looking better, are far healthier.'[4]

The press had a keen interest in the lifestyle of the modern girl. The volume of letters to the editor and commentaries about the modern girl indicated that the public wanted to know more and express their views about her lifestyle. For the editors of newspapers, she was the story. An article that appeared in the *Sunday Times* in 1925 seemed to confirm this. Miss Lilian Barker, the governor of the Borstal Institute for Girls at Aylesbury, gave yet another fillip to the popular subject of the modern girl when she spoke in vigorous defence of her:

There is, indeed, nobody more constantly and undeniably with us than this 'Modern Girl.' She has not yet, perhaps found her poet; but novelists, journalists and cartoonists are eternally employed in her advertisement, and without her help, the public speaker would, it is to be feared, often find him-self speechless. She should certainly be flattered by such universal attention to her most trivial actions. A change in the colour of her stockings sends her elders into mourning; the length of her skirt provokes European controversy, she crops her hair, and the philistines are upon her; when it grows shall not the pillars of the very Temple be shaken?[5]

The modern girl became a potent symbol of all that was changing during the interwar years. Her hairstyle, the clothes she wore, the nature of her work and her leisure activities were steeped with meaning and became signifiers of who the girl was. A report in a newspaper about a young girl being charged for a driving offence noted: 'arrested after one am. on April 15th in Baker Street, London on a charge of being drunk in charge of a motor car, Doris Neeves, a nineteen year-old girl with an Eton crop, was at Marylebone Police Court yesterday fined four shillings with five guineas costs'. The Eton crop told the readers something more about Doris Neeves other than her driving prowess.[6] Style became an important factor in defining the girl; the way that the modern girl styled her hair was the subject of much comment in relation to what it signified. While the Eton crop might be suggestive of girls who were rather wayward, bobbed hair gained the approval of Dr O. M. Holden, school medical officer in Dewsbury. In his annual report on school medical work, he took a practical view of hairstyles. He said that the fashion of 'bobbing of hair' in the case of young girls is to be encouraged; particularly in the poorer, less advantageously situated classes, bobbing the hair was a way to ensure cleanliness.[7] The point is that hairstyles became significant in defining the girl and, as such, judgements could be made about her. The modern girl was closely observed and commented upon. Among the reasons for the outpouring of anxiety regarding her leisure pursuits was her attraction to the growing commercial leisure industry and, more specifically, the cinema, dancing and fashion.

The girl came to epitomize what was considered wrong with the modern world and reflected wider insecurities that were manifested during the interwar years. The idealized girl in the background was rejecting that image and instead was becoming more visible in the public domain. She had a prominent place in the press where she was to be found in advertisements in newspapers and magazines, depicted as the girl smoking, the flapper, the dancing girl. These images were placed to encourage those reading the papers and magazines to buy into the image of the modern girl literally in terms of purchasing the products that enabled the girl to be modern. The image appealed to many girls for whom the idea of being seen as 'modern' gave them an air of confidence they would not otherwise have had and it enabled them to imagine that they had a higher status in society. The modern girl was distinctive in that she combined elements from a range of identities to create a persona with a cosmopolitan look. Importantly, she was found working in a range of different settings from the office to the factory; whatever her employment, she wanted to be part of the modern world. The lives of young girls were influenced by people who were unaware of their existence: Josephine Baker, Marlene Dietrich, Mary Pickford, Louise Brooks, Clara Bow, Lilian Harvey, Anna May Wong, Greta Garbo, Norma Shera and Pola Negri became their heroines. The modern girl was to be found in films, novels and advertisements; what she symbolized was sought after by the advertising industry that used her to promote a view of the new modern world. For example, an advertisement for Viking Chocolates had the following statement on the wrapper: 'The modern girl is no longer satisfied with old-fashioned rough chocolates with tasteless centres. Her better taste demands the perfection and variety of Viking Chocolates.'[8] The modern girl gave out mixed messages. She was clearly seen as someone who could influence others, and had high standards in terms of style, but she also unsettled what it meant to be a girl. The point was that people had a view about her. When Dame Ethel Smythe, the composer and suffragette, was interviewed the day after her seventieth birthday, she told the interviewer: 'I know a little about Jazz … but I dislike it extremely on the grounds that it makes no real contribution to music.' Speaking of the modern conditions she said, 'The modern girl is very jolly, and I like her. She is always polite, and always gives me a seat in the bus, tube or tram. But I think it is perfectly disgusting the way girls make up in public. It is a disgusting phase in the life of the modern girl which should pass.'[9]

The make-up that the girl chose to wear did provoke some stern views on the part of those who disapproved. The author of an article entitled 'Bitter Attack on Modern Girls' wrote that 'probably the bitterest attack ever launched upon the modern girl was made by Lady Frances Balfour in a debate with Miss Viola Tree at the London School of Economics, the subject: *is the young woman of today any worse off that she ever was?* Lady Balfour stated: "Her face is a mass of powder, her red lips are gashed out of all human resemblance, and the stinking reek of her makes me long for a breath of 'God's' sweet air." Miss Viola Tree was reported to have said very little in response.'[10]

The girl came into her own, taking up a dominant position in the leisure space that was created via the new leisure industries. Her visibility manifested itself through the choices she was making about how to spend her leisure time. Llewellyn Smith's observation that 'to-day the cinema is *par excellence* the people's amusement'[11] was an apt perception of its popularity; it was probably the most popular form of leisure during the interwar years. By 1939, the average weekly national cinema attendance was 23 million.[12] The introduction of the talkie improved the quality of the experience of going to the movies. Technological advances meant that, very quickly, continuous performances increased the potential to entertain more people in any one cinema; in fact, at the time of the

FIGURE 3 *Maid applying lipstick. Courtesy of Mary Evans Picture Library/ John Maclellan.*

NSL, cinemas were capable, via repeated performances, of entertaining well over a million people in London in a day.[13] This pattern of cinema attendance would have been replicated around the country. The doors opened from around midday until 11.00 pm and programmes were changed each Sunday.[14] It had become 'easily the most important agency of popular entertainment'.[15] Contemporary surveys provide an insight into the experience of going to the cinema. Rowson's survey noted that 43 per cent of all cinema admissions were for seats under sixpence and about another 37 per cent not more than ten pence; additionally, the bulk of cinemagoers were working class. Prices quoted were 5d. and 7d. for matinées and in the evenings either 5d., 9d., 1s. or 1s. 6d., although in working-class areas prices were between 4d. and 1s. before 3.00 pm.[16]

This was endorsed by the results of a study by Carr in the East End of London.[17] To understand why the cinema had such an impact, it is perhaps apposite to consider the impression made by a form of leisure providing what today might be considered the complete leisure experience. It was not so much the quality of the films shown, which on the whole were purely escapist, that appealed to the audience, but the whole experience of going to 'the pictures' was a form of brief liberation from the dreary physical surroundings that confronted many girls in their day-to-day lives. The early cinemas were rather spartan affairs, often in converted shops with the audience seated on benches. Alice recalled going to the picture house at the corner of Jamaica Road and Storks Road: 'We used to get an orange and some sweets, tuppence to go in and you got two films and it was all on the level and you didn't watch 'cause you couldn't see much but we enjoyed it.' Indeed, such was the poor quality of the environment of some cinemas that during a performance at the Star cinema in Abbey Street, Bermondsey one Saturday evening, a portion of the ceiling fell in and twelve members of the audience were injured.[18] The popularity of watching films was reflected in the use of venues such as town halls for film shows. As the period progressed and the cinema increased in popularity, the small venue gave way to larger lavish venues owned by a few major syndicates. The cost of installing sound equipment after the introduction of the Talkie in 1928 had been a factor in the decline of the small cinema. The 1920s witnessed what was considered the beginning of the great age of cinema building when ornate structures were designed. Cinemas were built like Chinese pagodas, Egyptian temples, Jacobean manor houses, Assyrian ziggurats and Spanish haciendas that attempted to make the audience feel that they were outdoors. What all these styles had in common was that they created a physical landscape in total contrast to the girls' everyday reality; they were living the fantasy. Many of the large syndicates had their own house style; for example, the Odeon group of cinemas adopted a style based upon the modern movement with streamlined curves, clean lines and art deco embellishments, and night-time floodlighting which enhanced the distinctiveness of the buildings. The 1930s saw the heyday of the super cinema with an ambience that was pure escapism. In fact, during the 1930s the Granada cinema, built in Tooting, south-west London, came close to developing the style of a cathedral. It had an Italianate entrance with Corinthian capitals and the interior was designed in a Gothic style, with a café and a huge foyer. Venues had plush seating and importantly they were heated. What all these styles had in common was that they created a physical landscape in total contrast to the girls' everyday reality; they were living the fantasy that they saw on the screen. An article written in *The Bermondsey Book*, a journal produced by those running an independent bookshop in Bermondsey with the intention of sharing culture with the local population, described the excitement of the cinema in the area: 'At night Bermondsey is unrivalled. Don't go to Paris, come to Bermondsey. It is at night a wonderful spectacle; Then the Picture Palaces burst force in a galaxy of light. Romance is portrayed on the posters which reveal the thrilling episodes of ladies driving Ford automobiles over cliffs and cowboys rescuing them with lassoes.'[19]

What the author was conveying was the power of the cinema not only in terms of the fantasy world of films but also the aura of the venue that made different worlds accessible to those living in an impoverished environment. For girls living in areas like Bermondsey, this was like entering a dream world. The impact that the architectural design of these cinemas had was evident in the essays produced for an essay-writing competition organized by the Girls' Friendly Society, with the theme of the essays entitled 'The cinema.' Miss Plumer, who had judged the essays, pointed out how important the cinema was in girls' lives in terms of their outlook on life. She stated: 'Practically every essay mentioned the effect created by the beauty of the cinema; not just luxury, but the enjoyment of the flowers, the shaded lamps and thick carpets.'[20] With such architectural designs came a social hierarchy of cinema venues.[21] The changing style of venue from the early days to the new large cinemas that were modern and luxurious had created a new concept of the experience of going to the cinema. These 'super cinemas' were not only to be found in more affluent areas of London, but Commercial Road in Whitechapel boasted the third largest cinema in London while the Elephant and Castle in Southwark, the adjacent borough to Bermondsey, had two super cinemas. The cinema was significant in that, according to contemporary surveys, the audience in the main comprised women and young girls,[22] providing them with some sense of escapism from the realities of their lives. It was not only the films that attracted girls to the cinema – as well as watching the films, the physical space was important for girls. The luxurious settings of the physical space often included cafés that added to the ambience and would have appealed to those who lacked the space within their homes to meet up with friends. Dance bands, Wurlitzer organs and orchestras provided music, which gave added impetus to the experience of going to the pictures: for a relatively small sum of money girls could step into another world. Access to space was important for the working classes in the absence of space at home. Fowler has emphasized that the cinema was a place of socialization, taking on many of the functions of the 'monkey parade.'[23] While Enstad has suggested that the cinema created a new public space which was uniquely open to women,[24] Rooff observed in 1935 that cinemas were comfortable, cheap and attractive and thereby a good meeting place. She noted that the films were sometimes an incidental feature in that the cinema was somewhere to go.[25] This was confirmed in oral testimony such as Lil's comment: 'There wasn't much difference between all the cinemas, it was just somewhere to go wasn't it?'[26] This was certainly the case for teenage girls during the period, but it was different for women who had responsibilities as wives and mothers. The results of a survey carried out by the Women's Health Enquiry Committee indicated that when married women talked about the limited time they had for leisure, they made the point that they very rarely went to the cinema.[27] This was in part due to the never-ending nature of their working lives within the home. It was the younger generation of working-class girls who took advantage of the opulent style and accessibility of the cinema. In trying to reinforce the idea that the cinema was accessible to all, James Wellard's comment sums up the levelling that the cinema potentially held: 'What does it matter if you work in a black-lead factory all day, if you can go and see Rudolph Valentino in the evening?'[28] Girls around the country went to the cinema as often as they could, using a variety of methods to gain entry. For those who were living in overcrowded homes, it was a space to meet and socialize, and for others the films they saw were important as they became visual resources to make use of in order to be up to date with the latest fashions. Whatever the reasons, their choice of how to spend their leisure time was not always approved of by the older generation or those outside their social class. Their disapproval reinforces the problematic nature of defining leisure in that the concerns expressed were not only about the activity that girls were engaged in, but they also related to the meaning that girls made of that activity. The meaning of an activity is contingent upon a number of factors that resonate with individuals in different ways.

Another major form of commercialized leisure that vied with the cinema for popularity among girls was dancing which, like the cinema, owed much of its sudden momentum to transatlantic influences. From the early part of the twentieth century, the impact of music from America was felt across Europe. By the 1920s, ragtime and jazz had taken hold of the popular imagination. The new syncopated rhythms brought about an urge for more freedom in dancing and for new dance forms. The pre-war period had already seen the introduction to England of the Tango, but with the new music came the new jerky, energetic dances, such as the bunny-hug, the crab-step, the kangaroo-dip, the Charleston, the horse-trot and turkey-trot which all became popular imports in England. They were a reaction against the inhibited movement of dancing in the past and were often seen as risqué; the bunny-hug was considered particularly indecent and had been banned in America for some time. While girls from all social classes took to the music and new dances, it did not accord with everyone. The extravagant steps and postures of many dances attracted disapproval and disgust from the older generation. Mr William O. Murray, assistant organist at Gloucester Cathedral, when asked what he thought of jazz music replied: 'Jazz is positively immoral, appealing as it does to the basest in human nature.'[29] Buckman has suggested that these dances became a form of rebellion for the younger generation who had the physical energy to perform them.[30] An article entitled 'The Mania of the Moment' reported: 'Every sort and kind of girl and boy dance: all have been caught up in the enveloping wave of dancing which is sweeping across the country. The Fox-trot, the One-step and the Boston are the ballroom dances of the moment.' One of the chief reasons given for the popularity of dancing was that it was cheap.[31] Many of these new dances were crazes that went out of fashion as quickly as they came in, or evolved into something that was more long lasting. As the period progressed, the styles of dancing and the music changed. The 1930s saw the development of contrasting styles of dance. In a reaction to the exuberance of the previous decade, there was a growth in dancing schools where steps, posture and movement were formalized. Ballroom dances such as the waltz, the fox-trot and the quickstep were particularly suited to this treatment, and what became known as the English style, smooth, elegant and stylish, emerged. The classical ballroom dance once again placed the girl in a position of being led by her male partner.

While this was occurring, many girls were dancing the Lindy hop, soon to be called the Jitterbug, which was set to the rhythms of the new swing music. These dances defied the set movements and instead improvised with a degree of physical energy and stamina that some of the older generation lacked. What this reveals is that energetic dances that the older generation disapproved of were prevalent before rock and roll emerged in the 1950s, or the emergence of the Twist in the 1960s. An interesting development towards the end of the interwar period was the novelty dance. The Lambeth Walk, which made its debut as a dance in the London-based musical play *Me and My Gal* in 1937, was quickly taken up by all classes, although in the play it was a dance for London costermongers. Samuel and Light have suggested that the wide acceptance of the dance is paralleled with the plot of the play where social barriers are broken down and aristocrats behave like cockneys and cockneys attempt to behave like aristocrats.[32] The new dance crazes were embraced by a wide cross section of society, and it has been suggested that in some ways it democratized dancing.[33]

The accessibility of these dances meant that the working classes were able to reach outside the parameters of their own social class when participating in dancing; it might have been in different venues but they were dancing the same dances. This was especially made possible with the advent of the Palais de Danse, the first such venue opening at Hammersmith in London in 1919 to host dance bands. The popularity of jazz was confirmed when in November of that year the Original Dixieland Jazz Band began a nine-month engagement at the Hammersmith Palais. By 1933, there were twenty-three such venues in London which provided an opportunity to indulge in the latest dance crazes and to gain access to an imaginary landscape conjured up by the plush surroundings of the Palais that had previously eluded the working classes if they wanted to go dancing. The Palais opened each night and charged one or two shillings entry fee. It had a balcony café, competitions and exhibition dances and, most importantly, a well-sprung dance floor. Like the films seen at the cinema, dancing at the Palais was a temporary escape from the reality of girls' lives and as such it became an important part of their leisure activities. A study carried out in 1941 found that, of twenty-seven girls between the ages of fourteen and seventeen who were interviewed, dancing was the most popular activity.[34] As well as these large plush venues, many local clubs began to have particular evenings when they hired small bands for dances, thereby enabling a wider range of socio-economic groups to afford to go dancing. The popularity of dance music with the public was confirmed in 1926 when the British Broadcasting Corporation decided to broadcast live music by Band leaders such as Jack Payne who attracted a large following. Girls became eager to know more about their film and music idols and many of them joined fan clubs that became popular during the period. Jessie recalled:

> Roy Fox was my favourite. I belonged to his fan club, used to go over the water to have a meeting,[35] you used to have late dance music on the radio and they'd play a new song and I'd scribble down all the words I could and then after a little while you sort of got to know it and then I think Jenny who was my friend was there and she used to try to take down the words so what I missed out she had and that's how we learnt all the modern songs. … I joined his [Roy Fox] fan club 'cos I liked him I don't even know where I got the information from. I used to write to a chap in Scotland he run the fan club he was the originator I suppose and he used to write and tell us all what was going on. I won a prize, well I didn't win it I got a consolation prize they wrote to ask why do you like Roy Fox? I got a huge big photograph of him head and shoulders and that was a consolation prize but I took it in work … and I had it varnished beveled and I used to put it in the bedroom. Every time I looked around the room all I could see was him looking at me. Roy Fox. I used to go and see him occasionally. I was the only one of my friends in the fan club I didn't like to tell them I was crazy about Roy Fox, I thought it was nothing to do with them it was something I wanted to do.[36]

Girls also worshipped the stars of the films that they saw and they often formed clubs that took the name of their 'favourite' star of the moment, such as the Garbo Club or the Navarro Club.[37] Some girls wrote to Hollywood or Elstree for signed photographs of the stars. Such was the importance of the film star for girls, that their worship of stars was a constant theme when discussions took place throughout the period on the part of social commentators concerning the impact of the cinema on young people. At a meeting of the Branch Presidents, Secretaries and Associate Workers of the Girls' Friendly Society it was suggested that they should reinforce the idea of discussing with girls in clubs the undesirability of star worship.[38] These organizations were aware that girls were making their own choices about how they wanted to use their leisure time; what made life interesting for many girls was the fantasy world to be found in the films they saw, rather than what the clubs had to offer, which for them was a fantasy but one they were disinclined to buy into.

Another area of rapidly expanding commercialized leisure that attracted girls' attention was the popular magazine industry. An indication of its growth between 1920 and 1945 is reflected in the fact that some sixty new magazine titles came on the market.[39] What was significant about this proliferation of magazines is that they acted as a powerful means to construct, disseminate and reinforce different notions of feminine identities that were often competing and contradictory. The development of magazines specifically for girls was a commercial response to the existence of an identifiable group of consumers in girls of all social classes. C. L. White has drawn attention to the way that these magazines were differentiated on class lines with the majority of those for the working classes being of a particular style, aiming at entertainment and mainly featuring pulp fiction, romance, glamour, sensation, lurid love stories and mysteries.[40] This genre included titles such as *Red Star*, *Secrets* and *Lucky Star*. Another genre was the schoolgirl magazines which had an emphasis on school stories, hobbies, friendship and leisure. While the industry attempted to target its publications at girls of different social classes, there was no guarantee that the magazines reached the targeted group only.[41] The fact that the readership of specific magazines was not always confined to those for whom they were intended would have had a bearing on the ways that the ideological messages implicit in the magazines were incorporated. For example, *Peg's Paper* was aimed at mill girls, and dealt with tales of romance, sensation and mystery, and offered an imaginary escape from the repetitive and arduous jobs that many prospective readers were engaged in.[42] It was one of a group of publications that Tinkler categorized as 'mother and daughter magazines', identifying a need on the part of girls and an older generation for an escape from the reality of their daily lives.[43] The limited power over their readership on the part of the proprietors is illustrated well by Clara's experience.

She read a lot when she was not at work; her favourite magazine was *Billy Bunter* whose target audience was lads, while her grandmother enjoyed reading *Peg's Paper* which was targeted more at young girls.[44] The popularity of reading magazines provides a good example of the complexity of what constitutes leisure. For some girls, reading magazines would have been a collective activity with their friends, devouring the fashions, latest styles, stories about their heroes and heroines; for others, this might have been a solitary activity, one which was not location bound and had a subliminal impact as it was a brief activity. What is interesting about these magazines is that while they may have differed in content, there were similarities in their style and the messages that they put across. Girls were more likely to succumb to the glossy images of the film stars and the latest fashions that were emphasized in some magazines, rather than those that located women in the home environment. While there was an intention to exploit their interest in the cinema with titles such as *Woman's Film Fair*, which featured articles predominately on beauty tips, fashion and news from the film world, other magazines dwelt on romance and fiction; however, stories were not the only subject matter contained in magazines.

The production and consumption of what the magazine had to offer was complex. Although magazines addressed girls' interests and were instrumental in defining who the 'girl' should be, these publications included a range of material such as hints on hobbies, sewing and knitting or aspects of keeping a good house, all of which reinforced the centrality of the domestic sphere in a subliminal way. Beddoe has suggested that the media projected stereotypical images of women and played a forceful role in the shaping of women's lives by reinforcing the idea that their role was firmly that of housewife and mother.[45] She has made the case that this was all-pervasive throughout the period. This may well have been their ultimate destiny; however, for a short time, girls were able to think otherwise. What became evident throughout the period was that there was not a coherent image of what constituted being a woman. The eventual role of girls as housewives and mothers would have been class specific and as such held very different prospects. Equally, girls from different parts of the country would also have had a different experience of becoming a woman. The magazines that proliferated at the time gave contrasting representations of women, very often in the same magazine. In some respects, the magazines in the early part of the interwar years affirmed the ways that contradictory messages about women's identity were defined in the wake of post-war reconstruction. This was mirrored and reinforced by both the verbal and visual texts to be found in magazines, the sales of which flourished at the time. Examples of this are to be found in the more popular titles of the period, such as *Good Housekeeping* (first published in 1922), *My Home* and *Modern Home*, both of which were first published in 1928, which had, as the titles indicated, an overt emphasis that firmly located women in the home environment. Yet other equally popular titles that proliferated at the time, such as *Women's Film Fair*, *Secrets*, *Red Star* and *Girls' Cinema*, emphasized the glamour of womanhood with helpful hints for all to achieve such images which were definitely intended to take women and more specifically teenage girls out of the domestic environment metaphorically. To give an example, *Girls' Cinema* included columns such as Fay Filmer's Film Chat, a monthly column called fashion fancies which promoted what was seen as the latest fashions, and stories with titles such as 'Shown up by her family', a story about a girl who tries to better herself, and 'Bondage of Barbara', a splendid story of a girl's self-sacrifice. *Miss Modern*, launched in 1930, sought to be all things to its readers, but it was obviously aimed at an older age group. In the December issue of that year there were several articles on choosing a husband from the then Duchess of York, 'a model for every wife and mother throughout the world', to one on choosing a partner by birth stars. Stories included one where a parlour maid wins the affections of a film star incognito, perpetuating the hope that the girl could possibly win the affections of a film star – if only she could meet one. Stories abounded that gave girls the possibility that perhaps they might achieve what they considered to be a dream and meet someone from outside of their social class who would transport them into another world. It was just a dream. The edition also included five pages of gossip and photographs of stars of the screen, stage and sport, a sheet of music for 'Miss Modern Foxtrot', and hints on slimming, make-up and exercise.

In these features, the magazine trod a narrow path between the established image of womanhood and the girl looking for excitement and glamour. Reinforcing concerns for physical appearance were the advertisements that totalled over one hundred, roughly half of which dealt with health and beauty. These advertisements addressed a much wider audience and age range; banishing grey hair, varicose veins and deafness were likely to be directed at a much older group than the girl. Alongside a number of advertisements dealing with beauty aids and make-up, there were several on slimming, one on bust development and two on increasing height. *Miss Modern*, despite its title, firmly led its readers along the traditional path of wife and motherhood, with some concessions to caring for appearance, romance and excitement. The beauty hints and the advertisements were aimed at making the appearance of girls fit into a certain mould – slender, well dressed (clothes were advertised for purchase by weekly payments), ready to attract the male. Often, the advertisers seemed more in touch with the practical detail of girls' lives than the stories and the articles to be found in many magazines. The advertisements, moralistic stories, as well as the home and beauty tips to be found in these magazines aided the cultural transmission of notions of girlhood and femininity throughout the period.[46] It is ironic that while this reinforcement of norms of femininity was affirmed on the part of the commercial leisure sector, those providing so-called philanthropic leisure for girls perceived the commercial leisure sector as a threat in terms of giving teenage girls unrealistic ideas about who they could be and, alongside government agencies, campaigned vigorously against a perceived threat from the commercial leisure sector to corrupt youth in terms of giving them unrealistic expectations of a lifestyle other than that of wives and mothers.

While it might have seemed that the commercial leisure sector was trying to reinforce a specific image of the girl that challenged who she was expected to be, the imagery to be found in the commercial leisure sector did not seriously challenge the future role of girls as wives and mothers, so much as make it appear more attractive via the lure of modern appliances that would seemingly make life in the home easier. The potential impact of the contradictory messages that were mediated by the leisure industry generally was recognized by contemporary writers such as Durant.[47] Tinkler has suggested that the proliferation of magazines indicated that women were recognized as a distinct market within which there were specific groups that could be targeted.[48] Advertising played an important role in reinforcing the image of the modern girl. Holtby drew attention to the power of advertising in guiding girls about the latest fashions. Making reference to the catalogue published by Messrs Harrods of Knightsbridge for January 1934, she referred to the 'Fashion Forecast' and noted the contents:

> Women are going to be their normal feminine selves in 1934. Parisian dressmakers have decided in favour of a sweetly feminine silhouette for the coming spring which will accentuate a woman's charm by means of ruffles, frills and other delightful artifices. Square shoulders, with their angular effects, will give way to soft fullness lower in the arm. Even evening gowns, boasting bare shoulders, will have a suggestion of sleeves or a deep frill beneath which the arms will be discreetly covered in quite a prudish manner.[49]

Working-class girls might not have been reading the Harrods catalogue, but the fashion forecast would eventually filter down to them and they would know what they would be expected to wear as a modern girl. But some girls may well have been literally at the cutting edge of cutting and creating the latest garments in the local factories that the well-dressed girl would soon be wearing. Fashion epitomized a sense of emancipation. In response to the forecast she gave, Holtby spoke of 'the post war fashion for short skirts, bare knees, straight, simple chemise-like dresses, ... cropped hair and serviceable shoes waging a defensive war against this powerful movement to reclothe the female form in swathing trails and frills and flounces to emphasize the difference between men and women'.[50] In doing so, she was celebrating the freedom that modern fashions had given to girls and women and was decrying the return to fashionable styles that might stifle the modern girl.

Hairstyles and the clothes that the modern girl wore became powerful signifiers of a challenge to what constituted femininity at the time. The period after the First World War was seen by some as a time when they thought that the world as they knew it was collapsing.[51] Reading a paper entitled 'The Psychology of the Female Mind' at a meeting of the Victoria Institute at the Central Hall Westminster, Dr Alfred T. Schofield suggested that the woman of early Victorian days had nearly disappeared but he thought she might still be found in remote parts of the country, describing her as 'gentle, quaint, prim, yet graceful'. The new woman he described as 'having the candid and clear look of complete emancipation'.[52] By the mid-1920s, femininity had become identified with simple unadorned youthfulness, rather than the ladylike ideals of the nineteenth century. It had also become associated with a certain type of personality; exuberance had replaced modesty and reserve.[53] The success of the commercial leisure sector was not simply a result of the glamour it offered teenage girls, it was also in part its accessibility. The different aspects of commercial leisure fed off one another. The cinema maintained its popularity partly due to the rapid turnover of films shown and the plush surroundings, but also because of the proliferation of information about the lives of the film stars of the day which was disseminated via many of the magazines that became popular at the time. The relationship between fashion and the film industry was also disseminated via these magazines. Girls got many of their ideas about style from the films they saw and the articles they read which told them more about the latest fashions. For example, *The Girls' Cinema*, first published in 1920, contained pictures of scenes from the movies, stories that had been made into films, articles about fashion and style, gossip about the Hollywood stars, information about fan clubs and competitions. The popular music of the day that girls danced to at the dance halls was also played at the cinema either by the bands in the café area or otherwise on the Wurlitzer organ. In many respects, the modern girl was constructed in and through the media and this is what caused disquiet. Outwardly, the modern girl might have looked as though she was emancipated but, as historians have noted, there were continuities in women's subordination within the home and the girl knew this was her destiny.[54]

The appeal of what the commercial leisure sector had to offer was not lost on the part of many large companies and factories that provided social clubs for their workers, which proved very popular with young people. Priestley, for example, observed that at Cadburys at Bourneville, 'The factory is almost as busy in the evening as it is in the day-time.'[55] At Peek Frean in Bermondsey, workers had access to a sports ground and games room, and dances were held on a regular basis. At the social committee it was noted that they held dances every Wednesday and they were very popular with a large attendance.[56] Those who arranged the dances clearly took into account the music that the employees would like. In 1923, it was advertised that Frank Hall's Syncopated Orchestra would be playing at a dance held there.[57] Girls had access to a rifle range and it was noted in the house journal that they had beaten the boys in a shooting match.[58] Like many large companies at the time, Peek Frean had a staff magazine entitled *The Biscuit Box*; by the third edition in January 1919, it had a section called 'Feminine Chatter' which discussed fashion and boyfriends among other things. In factories where the supervisors were not too strict, girls working on the production line were able to link work with leisure by sharing gossip about film stars and the latest fashions. Some companies also organized what was known as a 'beano' for their employees, which consisted of a day trip often to the seaside paid for by the employees but organized by the company. In some factories, a range of leisure facilities were provided for young people generally with more gender-specific activities for girls. Sports clubs became popular with girls within many localities, some girls joining cycling, tennis or swimming clubs. The local Labour Party in Bermondsey recognized the need to cater for leisure and was particularly acute to what teenage girls wanted in their leisure time. It offered an array of different pursuits that would appeal to the modern girl. By June 1921, the Bermondsey Labour Party reported that it had formed a sports club offering netball for women[59] and women's cycle races were advertised in the same journal. Despite dancing not always being seen as the right sort of leisure, the local Labour Party in Bermondsey acknowledged its popularity and regularly held dances at the town hall with bands that appealed to young people.

It would be wrong to assume that once commercialized leisure became more readily available, girls made no use at all of other forms of leisure. In the same way that they made use of commercial leisure as a means of gaining entry to images and identities outside of the realm of their social class, so too did they make use of other forms of leisure purely for utilitarian purposes. The policies of the Labour Party had a direct impact on the leisure available to the residents of Bermondsey, particularly through its efforts to promote educative leisure. It was one of the first boroughs to adopt the Public Libraries Act in 1850. By 1925, it had over 40,000 volumes representing a wide range of subjects.[60] It contained a reference library, reading rooms with periodicals, including trade and technical papers, and it also had a special section for visually impaired readers. There was an open access policy that enabled users to browse and discover new areas of reading material. Lectures were organized by the Public Libraries department in the winter months, which took place at the libraries, and it was noted that many young people attended these events; an example which proved popular was a talk entitled 'Flying around the world'.[61] In June

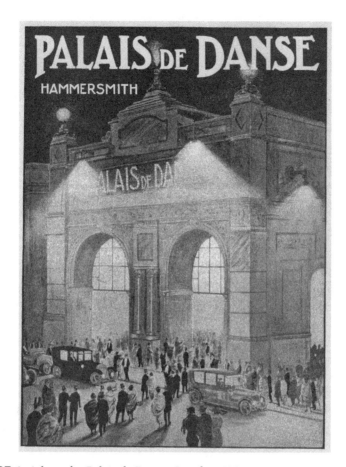

FIGURE 4 *Advert for Palais de Danse, London 1921.*

1931, an article about the local library stated: 'Whatever might be said about the increasing lack of serious purpose in our British democracy or the growing craze for amusement amongst modern folk it has to be admitted that the Bermondsey public is reading more widely as reflected in growing use of the library.'[62] This was supported by the fact that in July 1927 it was reported that there had been 339,084 recorded issues of books during the previous twelve months and the reading rooms were visited by 600,000 people per year.[63] In March 1927, it was reported that 7,000 people had attended a picture exhibition at the Central Library, and by May of that year the number who had visited the exhibition had increased to 11,786.[64] Although there is no breakdown of the profile of those visiting the exhibition, many who attended would have talked about their visit to others and, in doing so, shared their experience with a cross section of people. While girls were going dancing and attending the cinema, some were also making use of the library:

I was happy with me nose in a book. I got me books from the library Grange Road library it was a good library smashing library then.

I used to go to the library, they were good, I used to go to the Rotherhithe library, and you went in there and picked your book and it was all in lines with the numbers on you know and you say 'I want this book' and they take the number out and stamp the book and that's how they do it.

I belonged to the libraries it was wonderful our library was in Spa Road which is now offices. I virtually lived in that library, went there at a young age. If I was engrossed in a book and my mother called me I'd never hear. She used to throw things at me to get attention. ... I used to chase the girls round when she was putting the books back on the shelf in case it was one of my favourite authors was, it was mainly about schools you know boarding schools, I think It was Oxenburg I don't know if its the right one?[65]

Lil, who grew up in a working-class family in Bermondsey, recalled her taste in reading during her youth: 'I liked the boarding school stories because of all the tricks they got up to.' It is highly unlikely that Lil or any of her peers would have had experience of life at a boarding school to identify with, but the interest was in the fantasy of the story. A problem that publishers had to contend with was that girls had relative freedom of choice when they went to the library; providing the library stocked the book, they would in time get to read it. Ultimately, the publishers had no control over the use and interpretation that girls made of what they read, neither did they have control over the extent to which girls viewed the subliminal messages implicit in the magazines as a reality that could be attained, or simply a form of escapism that was to be savoured.

Increasingly, girls were seen to be participating in what were considered to be male sports. For example, girls who wished to play football had positive role models from girls' football teams that had been set up at factories and had become very popular. Perhaps the best-known team was Dick Kerr's Ladies, named after the factory where the girls worked. Such was their popularity that on Boxing Day 1920, 53,000 spectators went to Goodison Park to watch them play. Despite their large following, ironically they challenged notions of femininity and unsettled gender relations. The Football Association, expressing concern that the game was unsuitable for girls, stated: 'Complaints having been made as to football being played by women, the Council feel compelled to express their strong opinion that the game of football is quite unsuitable for females, and ought not to be encouraged ... and they should be discouraged from playing football.'[66] As a result, they were banned from playing at Football Association-affiliated grounds. Wrestling was another sport that had come to be perceived as a male sport. A newspaper article in 1928 entitled 'Girl Wrestlers form a Club,' was keen to affirm the respectability of this club by emphasizing that Miss Bina Theodore, one of half a dozen women who had formed a club in London, was 'a girl Bachelor of Arts', another member a teacher of ballroom dancing, a third a secretary.[67] The rapid rise in the popularity of commercial leisure and its particular appeal to young people presented challenges to the long-established providers of leisure. Increasingly, there was a divergence between what girls wanted from leisure and what the voluntary sector in particular had to offer. Bagatelle, ping-pong, sewing and choral singing no longer held their attention as they once may have. In a similar vein, faced with the choice of an evening at the local club hall or an evening at a plush cinema or dance hall, many girls chose the latter. In an article in *The Girls' Friendly Society Magazine* in 1920, the writer spoke of young girls as 'out for a good time and all the pleasure they can have'.[68] Throughout the period there was a gradual acknowledgement on the part of club workers that the club was not providing the sort of leisure that many teenage girls wanted. Miss Newby, the writer of an article in *The Girls' Club Journal* entitled 'The needs of girls to-day', noted that adolescent girls were 'all agog for new experiences' and that all girls wanted was to have adventure. Given the drab lives they were forced to lead, this might seem quite understandable. 'This sense of life comes to them as they swing to music. ... They get in the life of the street, reading thrilling stories at night. There is no half measure, life is satisfying or it is not. She is "fed up" or "bored stiff."'[69] Her comments endorse Willis's suggestion that youngsters preferred commercialized leisure rather than youth clubs where similar things were on offer, because there was an edge of social danger in terms of social relations in the commercial sector. He suggested that the commercial sector responded to customers' desires without the moral constraints of the youth club.[70] Throughout the interwar period, the cinema continued to be the focus of concerns on the part of those working in the voluntary sector. An article discussing the effects of the cinema claimed that young people were attracted by the high salaries and notoriety of stars: 'Most normal young people long for notoriety of one form or another and when they read of the doings of this and that personage on the films in every paper they pick up ... they are fired with ambition to be one themselves.'[71] The author went on to explain that it was not only the desire to be a film star that attracted young people:

> Many of them, especially girls, are influenced by the type of life that is depicted in most films. ... The women they see on films are, for the most part, living lives in which thrills and excitement play a large part. Consequently their whole idea of life becomes distorted, and they are fired with the ambition to live their lives as the women on the films seem to live theirs.[72]

Certainly, the cinema and dance hall proved to be stiff competition for the club and the education institute. For example, the Log Book of the Cosway Street Women's Institute in central London records comments about the large number of picture palaces and other cheap forms of amusement in the neighbourhood that increased the difficulty of getting people to attend classes.[73] It was clear that girls were asserting themselves and making choices, and in doing so, they forced those organizing rational recreation via the club to reconsider what constituted leisure. The compromises that had to be made on the part of the clubs were the subject of much discussion that was evident in their journals. In January 1934, a question had been raised at a gathering of the Girls' Friendly Society as to whether the organization had outlived its usefulness.[74] A response to this question appeared in *The Workers' Journal* the following month. Having noted that it was sad to hear the continuous fall in membership, it was pointed out that the majority of branches were not meeting the requirements of present-day girls. The Girls' Friendly Society was still perceived as an organization for servants on whom they had originally focused their attention. The writer (Veritas) stated: 'The old pre-cinema domestic servant is dying out, for her successor, with her one free evening a week, the attraction of the cinema is irresistible – there she meets boys and forms ties with which she thinks will lead to greater freedom for which she craves!'[75] *The Girls' Club Journal* recognized that the changing industrial landscape had implications for the nature of girls' leisure and the need for change. Talking of their developmental work, it noted: 'Girls of the future are likely to have much more leisure than the girls of to-day. Club work must change to meet the new conditions.'[76] Providing some advice in the *Girls' Club Journal for Club Workers* about running a junior club for those aged thirteen to sixteen, the author noted that this was a difficult group to work with as they would have left school at the age of fourteen and therefore not had any controlling influence. It was pointed out that although the girl was still a child, she felt grown up, she worked long hours, her work was monotonous and after work she expected freedom, pretty clothes, pocket money, choice of her own mates; it was a time she might well give up attending the club. It was suggested that it would be a good idea to encourage her to widen her interests: 'Often a girl's only idea of how to spend her leisure is to go to the pictures, or to stand on street corners gossiping with her mates, hoping to pick up a "feller."'[77] What the observer did not recognize was that for girls this could be a source of pleasure and a sign that she had the maturity to make her own choices. Some organizations such as the National Organization of Girls' Clubs were more alert than others to the fact that membership of their clubs would dwindle if they did not cater for the modern girl. This was evident in the debates within the voluntary sector about the need to provide mixed social evenings so that boys and girls would learn to co-operate with one another. Allied to this was also a realization that the image of the club needed to be improved in terms of physical space. It was acknowledged that better accommodation and facilities such as a canteen needed to be provided so that boys and girls could meet in decent conditions and natural circumstances that would provide them with the space to do something constructive.[78]

The intensity of the debates played out in the journals of these organizations reveals the tensions that were inherent in what they considered appropriate leisure to be and why many girls were choosing alternative ways to spend their leisure time. While compromises were made, in that clubs did organize specific evenings when girls could bring boys to the club, and they allowed modern dancing on some evenings for example, there were still concerns about aspects of girls' leisure that they did not approve of. The issue of how girls spent their leisure time resonated throughout the interwar period and such concerns were transmitted via the advice that club workers offered to them. Often, this advice was as much about what girls should not be doing as how they should behave. While it could be argued that the advice proffered was frequently based upon some form of social engineering, the roots of which were to be found in the philosophy of the philanthropic organizations of an earlier period, this was not necessarily always the case. For example, an article in *The Girls' Club Journal* in January 1928 stated: 'Our educational aim in our club should be to supply what is lacking in the social environment of the girls' homes and places of work, and to correct what is actually harmful and wrong.'[79]

Their aims arose from a historical awareness of the impoverished nature of the environment that girls lived and worked in. In the earlier part of the century, the club workers had monitored the hours that girls were required to work without a break and had campaigned on their behalf for better working conditions. In this context, it is understandable that they considered that leisure should be constructive and educative, in order to provide the opportunity for girls to be able to improve the quality of their lives. They therefore wanted leisure to focus on developing a sense of order and discipline in the lives of girls and, importantly, to reinforce specific notions of femininity that were mirrored in the activities that they provided for working-class girls. But for many girls the allure of what the commercial leisure sector had to offer seemed to provide the space for them to consider a range of alternative identities and, importantly, to have some fun. Needless to say, this created a tension within the voluntary sector; while some were convinced that the initial aims of their organizations were still of relevance, others thought differently. At the General Conference of the Girls' Friendly Society in 1938, Miss Mainprice, the London Secretary, spoke of the changing times and how girls didn't want things of the past. She argued that it must be accepted that times had changed and that the Girls' Friendly Society was faced with competition from other organizations.[80] While there was concern about the nature of the leisure that girls were drawn to, Mr Kennedy Cox from the Docklands Settlement in Bermondsey pointed out quite rightly that it was useless to expect any broadening of horizons from the home due to overcrowding and a lack of any privacy. He drew attention to the need for restrooms in clubs and, more significantly, for club workers to be aware of the difference between sitting and dreaming and loafing.[81] The latter part of his remark is interesting in terms of the language used in relation to what constitutes leisure. Sitting and dreaming could well be a respectable moment when the individual is dreaming of ways to improve her lot in life, something of which those who organized the youth clubs would approve, whereas loafing implies doing nothing, which in turn implies wasting time that would not be seen as a worthy pursuit.

A significant aspect of the changing lifestyle of girls throughout the period was the annual holiday. Even prior to the 1938 Holidays with Pay Act, many working-class girls did have an expectation of a holiday. Llewellyn Smith noted the increasing numbers of Londoners who were entitled to an annual holiday of at least a week on full pay; however, it was usual that the individual had to have been employed by the company for twelve months prior to the entitlement.[82] For those living in areas such as Bermondsey, this was problematic as much of the work available was of a seasonal and casual nature. Young people knew that as they neared becoming eligible for an adult wage, they were likely to be dismissed from their job, and the result of this was that there would have been a sizeable number of workers who did not qualify for the entitlement of a paid holiday. How holidays were spent was dependent to a greater extent upon available funds. When they had attended school, many girls would have had holidays provided by organizations such as the Country Holiday Fund or their school. Those who attended clubs run by the voluntary sector were often able to have a holiday organized by the club. Clara recalled attending a local club and being taken on holiday: 'We used to go away camping, Littlehampton we used to go. They was just ordinary people who run it mind you, they had money. You didn't have to pay it was free.'[83] The clubs also organized day trips: 'We had day trips to Littlehampton, Bognor, Clacton, Southend, Dymchurch. They were mainly through the club that we belonged to, Sunday-School trips, Band of Hope trips.'[84] For some girls, having contacts at the seaside or their friends knowing someone, meant that they were able to have a holiday. Lil was fortunate in this respect:

My friend's grandma had a boarding house down at Sandgate just beyond Folkestone, between Folkestone and Hythe and we had our first holiday without parents down at Doris's grandma's. I think there were about ten or twelve of us, how the poor old soul put up with it I don't know. I was about sixteen, seventeen. A whole week at the seaside was wonderful absolutely wonderful. You name it we did it 'cos the boarding house had back steps straight onto the beach so it was really fantastic. It wasn't my first holiday 'cos I'd had a holiday at the seaside with my Gran when I was a child that was also Folkestone. I went with my Gran and my Auntie. I suppose I must have been about seven or eight something like that.[85]

There were many youth hostels within reach of London where members could pay one shilling for a bed for the night. For those who could not afford an annual holiday, day trips were a possibility. Bank holidays became the time when large numbers of people set off for the nearest countryside or beach, and others were able to go on a boat trip along the Thames Estuary to Southend where they could visit the Kursal Pleasure Gardens, or Margate where they could go to Dreamland and perhaps go on the rollercoaster or scenic railway. Finding the funds for a family holiday was not always within reach of working-class families as not all workers received holiday pay, and even if they did their wage would not cover a holiday for all of the family due to the fragility of the family income.[86] A housewife interviewed for the NSL noted that 'the only way to get a few days off is through the dividend paid out by the Co-op. to members; ... should the money be wanted for something in the meantime, good-bye holiday'.[87] One respondent in the NSL, speaking about the stress of going on holiday and paying for it later, noted: 'We have only been on one holiday, we took other people's advice to go and afford it afterwards. It made a change for us, but I cannot say we enjoyed it, as the "affording afterwards" kept us worrying.'[88] This was certainly the case for families around the country. For many working-class families in Bermondsey and the East End of London who may well have been in this situation, their annual holiday took place in early September when often the whole family went hopping in Kent. Such was its popularity that the White Horse Club in Bermondsey closed during the hopping season.[89] It became a tradition for some families. 'Hop-picking is the holiday that we look forward to, and would not miss it for anything. We have three to four weeks away in the beautiful hop gardens of Kent and a finer holiday nobody could wish for. When the time is getting near, which is at the end of August or beginning of September, neighbours greet each other in the following way. "Hello! Going Hopping this year?"'[90]

The practice of going hopping draws attention to the definitional ambiguity of the boundaries between work and leisure. Most hop-pickers were women, and often they took the children with them and left their husbands behind to continue working. Despite working each day, the women felt that they had a holiday, yet once 'pull no more bines' was called, which signalled the end of the working day, the women would attend to the work they did in the domestic sphere, only it was in the hoppers' huts rather than their overcrowded homes. O'Neill noted that the level of work that mothers insisted their children had to do varied.[91] For many of those who went hop-picking regularly, it was considered a holiday, the difference being that they worked in the fields rather than a workshop or factory. For girls who were employed as casual or seasonal labour, the hopping season provided a respite from their impoverished surroundings. Recalling going hopping, the hard work was something that Emmy remembered: 'We went Hopping, you had to work picking the Hops, if you didn't work you didn't get a new pair of boots when you got home.' For girls growing up during this period, a new set of role models emerged that enabled them to challenge how they were defined and instead gave them the scope to define who they wanted to be. The problem was that this caused disquiet with the older generation across the social classes.

5

The imaginative consumer

It was shortly after mid-day that I began to walk to Jamaica Road,
factory girls were hurrying home arm in arm for an hours rest
and a meal, and the pavements were gay with the shimmer of
silk stockings, coats and their close fitting frocks with what the
modistes call 'an air'. Some of them had artificial pearl earrings,
and many had flowers pinned to their coats.[1]

Style was important for girls across the social classes during the interwar years. They were conscious about what they wore and much of their time was spent ensuring that they were up to date with the latest styles. They dominated cinema audiences, they were visible at dances and they embraced the new musical styles of the period. Working-class girls embraced their time for leisure with great enthusiasm and they were highly visible in the public sphere. What is of interest here is how they were able take up the cultural products of newer forms of leisure available to other groups of women given their limited disposable income. Within the historiography of leisure, a view has prevailed that suggests access to leisure was determined by the level of wages and the cost of living.[2] This has been a consistent line of thinking since the 1930s, as noted by Durant: 'Participation in leisure pursuits to-day is so much a question of possessing money.'[3] It was this assumption that formed the basis for locating the advent of a teenage consumer culture in the late 1950s, when young males were seen to have an increased disposable income that allowed them to spend their money on the products of a commercial leisure culture. In 1959, Abrams claimed that his research showed that there was 'distinctive teenage spending for distinctive teenage ends in a distinctive teenage world'.[4] His research pointed to the fact that working-class boys had high levels of disposable income due to improved earnings coupled with the decline in youth unemployment. While Abrams' findings might be subject to critique, there is no doubt that the essence of this comment informed contemporary understandings of the emergence of a teenage consumer culture, locating it firmly as a post-Second World War phenomenon. Although Fowler challenged the time frame for this development and made the case for the emergence of a teenage consumer culture during the interwar years, he continued to reinforce the theme of the increase in the wages of young male wage earners and the relatively low levels of youth unemployment as being the reason for a teenage consumer culture emerging during the interwar year.[5] This analysis is problematic in two major respects: first, the continued focus on young male wage earners with a lack of acknowledgement that young girls were wage earners too; indeed, as has been shown, they were much sought after in some industries and they were also highly visible in terms of their leisure activities. The second issue is the continued assumption that access to leisure was simply based upon levels of disposable income. It is interesting that, during the 1930s, Durant observed: 'Two things are certain. Youth and girls of the working class tend to spend more on the cinema, dances and clothes than seems to be compatible with the small total sum that they earn.'[6] This observation was endorsed during the same period by the findings of Harley's research into the leisure pursuits of teenage girls that established that working-class girls were actively participating in commercial leisure activities. When Harley interviewed girls about their leisure pursuits, she found that there was no difference between those who were in employment and those who were unemployed in terms of the leisure pursuits they engaged in. Reflecting on how this was possible, she suggested that parents possibly gave them money to fund their leisure pursuits.[7] Given the limited disposable income in many working-class families, this would have been highly unlikely. What it does suggest is the need for an alternative analysis which will provide answers to the question of how girls on limited means had the ability to go to the cinema so frequently, go dancing, were able to dress in the fashionable styles, wear the latest make-up and hairstyles and read the latest magazines.

Following Langhamer's assertion that 'the existing conceptual frameworks of leisure history are not appropriate to the study of women',[8] it is useful to move away from a framework that uses levels of disposable income as an indicator of the existence of a teenage consumer culture as it misses the point that access to the products of the commercial leisure industry was not solely dependent upon the availability of hard cash. Crucially, linking access to leisure with access to money fails to take into account, first, that there are subtle differences in purchasing and acquiring, and second, the act of purchasing or acquiring occurs in a social context and, as Enstad has suggested, becomes part of a collective culture.[9] These two factors are vital for developing an alternative reading that brings a more nuanced perspective to the development of a teenage consumer culture. The nature of purchasing and acquiring on the part of teenage working-class girls reveals the many strategies embedded in their class culture that were indeed utilized by their mothers for survival of the family purse, but were used by teenage girls for more pleasure-seeking purposes. This enabled them to resist being excluded from the newer forms of commercial leisure by virtue of their lack of money. Their actions are mindful of Clarke and Critcher's suggestion that the subordinate culture always has a number of strategies and responses in order to cope and resist.[10] In this instance, it is the nature of purchasing and acquiring that is of interest to this discussion. To understand how girls negotiated access to the leisure of their choice, there is a need to look at the immediate context within which they were living and also the wider social context in terms of changes taking place in society and the impact this had on them.

Attention has been drawn to the lack of analysis of the fabric of day-to-day life in the context of the development of leisure.[11] Yet it is the fabric of the day-to-day lives of girls that illuminates how they were able to gain access to leisure. It is useful, therefore, to explore the creative ways that girls were able to draw upon the normative behaviour of their class culture in order to adapt their cultural practices to their own social needs, in this case gaining access to commercial leisure. This will also allow for the symbolic meaning of their leisure activities in terms of identity to be explored. The common practice of handing over wages to their mother each week reinforces the idea that young wage earners were not entirely independent of the family; girls were still financially under the control of their parents.[12] The ratio of money given up each week seems to have been similar as reflected in comments such as: 'When I started working I got eight shillings a week. I think my mum used to take six shillings';[13] another respondent recalled: 'I earned ten shillings a week. I used to give my mum eight shillings.'[14] There were, however, differences as to what girls would have to buy out of their wages. Some girls had to buy all of their clothes from the money their mother gave back to them, while others who did not have to do this considered themselves quite lucky:

Well I was rather lucky really my mum used to buy all my clothes I never had a worry about anything, cushy life in a manner of speaking. So if I wanted anything ... I saved up. ... You couldn't save up for much not out of that money but me mum bought all my clothes so if I wanted anything ... she probably had a couple of bob behind her so that helped you know.[15]

The point was that girls had to be creative in the way they used their 'spends'. The popularity of the cinema with teenage girls was in no doubt. The frequency with which films changed at the cinema necessitated regular visits on the part of those who wished to keep up with the latest images on the screen. But, even attending the 'tuppenny flicks' that sprang up throughout Bermondsey proved to be beyond the means of many teenage girls, so to ensure that they had access to the latest films, they found alternative ways of gaining entry. 'It was a treat if you went to the pictures, you used to queue up or try and bunk in didn't you?'[16] Sarah explained the ease with which this could be done. 'You'd pay tuppence to get in, the tuppenny rush, or you'd bunk in, you know, round the side, you know those doors, you've only got to push them a bit and they'd open, and we'd all be in mixing with the crowd.'[17] This was reaffirmed by other recollections of how girls gained entry to the cinema while on a meagre wage. 'We used to go to the pictures four times a week, Saturday and Sunday, Tuesdays and Thursdays, if you couldn't get in then you'd bunk in.'[18] It was not only at the cinema where this technique applied, as Kathy recalled: 'I was always chancing something when we couldn't get in to a dance, What colour's the pass? Had some bus tickets I thought these are alright you couldn't tell when you go in. I got in.'[19] 'Bunking in' clearly illustrates how boundaries can be shifted within cultural formations to enable inclusion in wider cultural practices. Girls negotiated other ways to gain access to the commercialized forms of leisure, such as making use of boys to pay their entry: 'I went to the pictures, there was nowhere else to go was there? But only at the weekend when you got money or got someone to take you up there.'[20] By using these strategies, girls were challenging their subservient role in relation to men and taking control of the situation to suit their own ends. While they found ways to gain access to the cinema, the conditions in which they saw films at the local venues during the earlier part of the interwar period were often quite austere as the following comments attest: 'I remember going to the pictures, we'd go to the Old Kent, the one on the corner of Galleywall Road near Shuttleworths [a factory that made Chocolates]. Terrible in there it was, sitting on a wooden bench, nothing to rest your back on.'[21] Women often recollect having to sit in the cheaper seats, referred to as the Gods. 'I went to the Hippodrome sat in the Gods there, climbed up all them ruddy stairs, well that was all a treat and you used to have to go all the way round to the tunnel [Rotherhithe tunnel] to get ice cream 'cos there was a shop there which was cheaper.'[22] Despite the rather spartan accommodation, the important thing was that the cinema was a means by which working-class girls were able to see films that others in more affluent areas also saw. As the period progressed, entry to the larger and more luxurious venues was more expensive even for the cheaper seats, but this was not always seen as prohibitive:

> Sometimes we would go to the Super in Tower Bridge Road. There was a fairground there with swings and roundabouts before they built the cinema there, and there were still lots of rats about. Sometimes, we'd see people

just about to sit down in some of the best seats and we'd say 'don't mind us saying so, but there's a rat under one of those seats.' With that, they'd move away and then we'd pinch those best seats.[23]

Whether the physical conditions of the cinema were spartan or luxurious, the films themselves offered up a form of escapism from the monotony of girls' lives. The images on the screen provided ideas and fantasies which became part of their imaginative landscape; they also provided a repository for keeping up with the latest fashions. In many respects, girls' behaviour set them apart from the older generation as they were asserting their desire to have an identity other than that of wife and mother – albeit for a short period of time. Walton and Walvin suggested that many women found in the cinema one of the first collective escapes from home and industrial drudgery and in this sense it became a catalyst for social change in that conventional roles were challenged on the screen.[24] Certainly, this is supported by Bakke's study of the leisure pursuits of the unemployed during the period; he quoted two respondents who said of the cinema, 'I think that high society pictures are the best because they teach you how to be proper. … Pictures are my first choice because they make you think for a little while that life is alright.'[25] As with other areas of the country, girls in Bermondsey would have felt the resonance of the changing nature and attitudes towards leisure; the widening opportunities for leisure provided them with a glimpse of a world beyond their own locality. This would have been set against the harshness of their mothers' lives which was captured in a description by Jessie Stephen, a local councillor, who pointed to the limited time that women had for relaxation of any sort. Having set out the daily routine of the typical Bermondsey housewife, she explained: 'Occasionally she varies this monotonous round by going to the picture palace or a music hall with her husband, but it is rarely that she is found occupying the best seats.'[26] The modern girl had different aspirations, and Mitchell has suggested that by the end of the nineteenth century, girls' culture indicated that their lives would be different to their mothers' due to the influence of commercialization and the proliferation of advice given to young girls that gave them access to a wider range of models from which to glean an identity.[27] It is true that by the interwar years, girls on the whole were looking to the commercial leisure sector for entertainment and, importantly, advice about how to adopt the role of the modern girl. Certainly, they faced a complex array of messages in the advice given to them about all aspects of their lives, but they were selective about the advice they took on board. A reason why girls were often reluctant to listen to the advice offered by those in the Girls' Club movement was the fact that it did not fit with their ideas of how their time for leisure should be spent. Implicit in much of the guidance given by the philanthropic organizations was the concept of deferred gratification, but this was an anathema to those whose class culture had long taken on a fatalism concerning the future. Part of the problem that the Girls' Club movement had to contend with when giving out advice was that there had long been a suspicion on the part of the poor of the motives of those providing much-needed space to engage in leisure. Girls had a choice: they could seek advice about womanhood from the older established organizations or they could look to the advice being offered to the modern girl in the modern world that was mediated through the commercial leisure sector. This was often far more appealing to girls, as Alexander noted: 'Advertizing and the cinema playing upon fantasy and desire enabled women to *imagine* an end to domestic drudgery.'[28] This was certainly the case for many young girls. The advertising of the latest fashions that abounded at the time fed the desire of girls to copy the images they saw in the advertisements. Melman has suggested that many women would have escaped their reality by reading romantic fiction.[29] The images of women that the commercial leisure industry portrayed were clearly targeted at women at particular stages in the life cycle. They may have provided married women with a form of imaginary escapism from the drudgery of their lives, but, by virtue of their role in the domestic sphere, older women were limited in terms of the extent to which they could play out such fantasies or aspire to them. However, teenage girls found themselves in a different position, one that Hoggart, referring to this stage of the life cycle, likened to 'a brief flowering period'.[30] For girls, leisure had the potential to reflect and play a part in their gradual emancipation from a subservient role. Like married women, girls observed the possibilities that the images portrayed by the commercial leisure industry held; however, unlike older women, they had the resources to negotiate the means to have access to some of the images and styles portrayed in the commercial leisure sector.

The teenage working-class girl was faced with a number of contradictory images as she grew up; the idealized image of being a wife and mother which was constructed by those with little understanding of how this role could possibly manifest itself in an impoverished environment, and the variety of role models to be found on screen and in magazines. Heroines could be hard-headed business women, sweet young things or gangsters' molls; either way they were as much a fantasy as those images promoted by those in the voluntary sector that bore little resemblance to girls' lives. For teenage girls, romance and fantasy were much sought after, not because they seriously imagined life was like that, for as Elizabeth Roberts has suggested, young girls at that time were 'a conforming and conformist generation'.[31] What they were doing was resisting the role of wife and mother which they would eventually take on. While the cinema and advertising offered the girl an array of images of womanhood, it would be wrong to assume that it was a revolutionary force which liberated women from their traditional roles of wives and mothers. The messages it gave out were more complex; on the one hand, films presented a range of images which many social commentators thought would entice girls away from their role in the domestic sphere, yet a great deal of films also reaffirmed the image of women as wives and mothers. What was seen in the films was reinforced by images to be found in advertisements and stories in the many magazines that were published at the time. *Peg's Paper*, which was specifically aimed at working-class girls, included regular feature 'Peg Trots around Hollywood', which clearly played to fantasies of the working-class girl going to Hollywood. It also featured double-page spreads on film stars advising girls how to copy the style of the stars. Such glamorous images were there to be copied by those who wished to keep up with the fashions, and they became resources for teenage girls who extricated identities from the contradictory images they had presented to them. 'I got my ideas about fashions from the magazines, I've even come across, well bits of paper where I've seen written down what I've seen in a book. Oh I'll copy that down and when you went in a room you how to walk and all that sort of thing.'[32]

The phenomenon of the film star was created during this period. As Richards has pointed out, it was the stars whom the audience went to see as they set the fashions for hair and clothes, and he argued that the star represented an ideal to be admired and identified with.[33] Kathy recalled: 'I was about seventeen or eighteen, all for the fashions. I had two strips of hair here [pointing to fringe] and I had two bobs here like Pola Negri. And they used to call me Pola Negri and I dyed me hair, I used to see the fashions on the pictures.'[34]

The influence of the images portrayed on the screen was also noted in the NSL: 'Girls copy the fashions of their favourite film star. At the time of writing, girls in all classes of society wear "Garbo" hats and wave their hair á la Norma Shearer or Lilian Harvey.'[35] The local shops were quick to adapt in order to cater for the needs of the modern girl: Ben's Ladies Hairdressers in Bermondsey advertised Bobbing, Manicures, Shingling, Dyeing, Marcel Waving, Water Waving and Tinting.[36] The same hairdresser also offered weekly payments and was happy for clubs to be held, as the commission was good.[37] As the cinema became an important conduit that offered girls a range of representations from which to explore their identity, the power of the cinema to influence teenage girls was not lost on those working in the voluntary sector who were trying to persuade teenage girls of the benefits of physical training. An article written in 1936 by Olive Worsfold in the *Girls' Friendly Society Workers' Journal* entitled 'The Aims of Recreative Physical Training' attempted to set out an understanding of the attitudes of the present-day girls' towards physical training. In Worsfold's view, 'the girl' had a very utilitarian attitude towards physical training as she attended classes to make herself fitter, more beautiful and often slimmer. Worsfold attributed what she perceived as an increased interest in personal appearance to, first, the press, which had been full of articles and photographs of different types of exercise and keeping fit, the author of such articles often being a well-known star of stage or screen which increased the reader's interest; second, an aim on the part of young girls to be like the beautiful stars of the cinema; and third, the impact of cheap clothes. In relation to the latter point, Worsfold stated: 'To dress oneself well and fashionably nowadays is within the means of the majority of people, but at the same time the seams of cheap clothes allow of no letting out, and therefore we have to fit our figures to the clothes and not the clothes to our figures.'[38] It was not only the images to be found on the screen that presented possibilities of gaining access to the lifestyle of the rich and famous, but the venues themselves came to offer a dream space. In a similar way that teenage working-class girls gained access to the latest films, albeit in rather primitive surroundings during the early part of the period, they also found ways to gain access to the popular music of the day and to participate in the latest dance crazes. As McKibbin has noted, it was difficult not to be aware of the popular music and dances of the day.[39] Dancing, like the cinema, was seen as a means of escape and took place at a variety of venues from purpose-built dance halls to small club halls. To listen to the latest music, girls did not have to wait until a visit to the dance hall; instead, dance music could be heard on the wireless, the ownership of which became increasingly common throughout the period. Although rather primitive in some instances, wirelesses did enable the latest tunes to be heard, and many homes had what was known as a Crystal set:

> When I was fifteen me and Nell she had a sister Sally and she was courting and her chap was very, very, clever and he made … the Crystal set, the one with the cat's whisker. And on Saturday night her mum and dad always used to go out for a drink and … and we'd be in her house when we'd come home from a dance and we'd put the earphones on and find the cat's whisker and listen to Jack Hylton and we used to dance around to it.[40]

Many people made their own wireless, as Maude recalled: 'We used to have a wireless, our dad made his own wireless. He used to get the bits and pieces and make his own aerial and things. One day we put the wrong wire in the wrong place me and my brother, I said to him "If you put that on there it will go." He blew it up.'[41] The acquisition of a wireless became more accessible with the advent of hire purchase. Both national and local newspapers throughout the period advertised wirelesses for sale, and often older siblings who still lived at home purchased a wireless for family use, an indication perhaps of their marginally superior economic position. As the period progressed there was a greater demand for gramophones and records. The District Gramophone Supply Stores at Old Kent Road and Tower

Bridge Road placed an advertisement in the *Bermondsey Labour Magazine* advertising the fact that they had over 7,000 records for sale; the music catered for an eclectic range of tastes including melba, carusso, opera, organ music and dance music.[42] Gramophones were sold for cash or by instalments. Wirelesses and loud speakers were also on sale with easy terms available. Gramophones and records were also advertised in the *Bermondsey Labour Magazine* both new and second-hand priced at 4s. and 5s. 6d.; records cost 6d.[43]

There was more to dancing than simply knowing the correct steps for the latest dances: it was also about being dressed for the occasion. Many of those who grew up during the period recall buying special clothes which were the height of fashion to wear when they went dancing. This was especially so as many venues had a dress code:

> I know I had a dress made and it was a short front and it had a long back some lady made it for me, I think she made us four we all 'ad the same dresses and I can still see it, it was red with lovely roses on it, you know spread out like and oh we danced round we used to watch our finger we used to watch our skirts go out, you know.[44]

For some, the purchase of a dress like this was seen as an investment to be worn on many occasions, and it also affirmed that they could dress in the style of those outside their social class. 'I always wore a long dress for dancing. There used to be a shop called Half Guinea or Guinea Gown shop and that's where I bought me dress, course, you'd wear it for some time you know. Imagine twenty-one shillings for a dress.'[45] Certainly, the styles that working-class girls adopted symbolized their ability to participate in cultural practices in the same ways as girls from other social classes. Advertisements in magazines such as *Miss Modern* offered the purchase of fashionable clothes by instalments, which meant that the latest fashions were within reach of those on a low income. For girls, fashion provided them with pleasure and autonomy, and it allowed them to leave briefly the reality of their lives. Mowatt argued that the new fashions blurred class distinctions and this was indeed true.[46] While fashion had always been taken up in creative ways by working-class women to produce a sense of identity, the newer technology at this time with mass-produced patterns and off-the-peg clothes not only created a culture of demand for styles which those in other social groups wore, but more importantly it created the means to achieve them. It was not just the design of fashions which was taken up by woman of all social classes, other factors were involved too; the introduction of artificial silk rayon in 1921, which was cheaper than proper silk and importantly a good imitation, also increased the potential to recreate fashionable styles. It was during this period that the cultural signifiers of respectability became increasingly concentrated on consumer products. For many teenage girls, respectability was achieved by taking on the more positive image of the modern girl who had an air of glamour and independence rather than pursuing notions of respectability associated with what were seen as outdated images of the subservient young woman. Modern respectability was, in part, achieved by the clothes that girls wore; in fact, Meacham has suggested that clothes or lack of appropriate wear determined the extent of working-class social life.[47] Style of dress had always been an indicator of a level of respectability for working-class girls and this became an increasingly important signifier of respectability with the accessibility of the wealth of images advertised on the cinema screen and in magazines that could be copied. Fashion also became a means of crossing cultural boundaries in that individuals from different social classes could share similar leisure experiences via the symbolic meaning invested in fashion. The subtle divisions that the consumption of fashionable styles created served to reinforce the fragmentation that Johnson described as occurring in all aspects of social life including leisure.[48] Items of clothing had long been used as a means to judge levels of status and respectability across the social classes. While Booth described the flamboyant hats of the factory girls of the East End of London which set them apart from others,[49] the workers at the Cambridge University Mission in Bermondsey saw the hat as a marker of respectability when commenting upon the problem girls being hatless and boisterous.[50] Items of clothing took on a significance that was important, not only for those wearing the clothes but they signified to others a statement about who the individual wanted to be.

For teenage girls, going dancing not only involved wearing the right clothes but also having money for supper afterwards, the pie and mash shop being a substitute for the West End supper club:

Well then we used to go dancing quite a bit those days. ... I think every Friday night used to go to a dance, used to see all the girls walking along with an ordinary coat always wore a long dress for dancing that always amazed me afterwards. But it was always a good night and then when you came out you'd pop into Manzies [a local pie and mash shop] for your supper – it was only three pence.[51]

The ways in which girls prioritized what was important in relation to how they spent their leisure time were not always approved of. In a study carried out by Harris on the uses of leisure in Bethnal Green, an area in east London that had similar socio-economic conditions to Bermondsey, he referred to the boys and girls who, having just left school and started work, constituted a problem in terms of how they chose to spend their leisure time: 'and so while money is in their pockets, off they go to the cinema with the most lurid films, or to the dance halls where they can gratify their love for unhealthy emotion'.[52] While the leisure pursuits of teenage girls prompted commentators to accuse them of acting in a frivolous and irresponsible manner, their actions had a more serious meaning. The creative use of their own cultural practices to look smart and be up to date with the fashions of the day signalled that they were rejecting their subordinate position in society. By establishing their right to be part of the consumer culture, they were asserting their entitlement to have choice in their lives. The factory girls' clothes might have differed from those worn by wealthier girls in terms of quality of fabric and finish, but as fashionable styles became simpler and therefore easier to mass produce they could be bought off the peg, by mail order, by instalments or made at home. Magazines often had special bargain patterns on offer, and the advantage of mass-produced patterns was that they could be used again and again.

Throughout the period there is ample evidence, within the context of leisure, of girls seeking ways to take control of their circumstances and to form subjectivities based upon their limited resources. Some girls saw the workplace as a resource to be drawn upon. Alice, who started her working life as a trainee machinist, used her ingenuity in order to be stylish. She negotiated with her fellow workers to help enable her to wear the latest styles. The factory she worked for produced clothes for a high-class fashion house in the West End of London, allowing her to observe the latest fashions and to make use of her expertise in order to make her own clothes in the latest styles:

> You couldn't afford to buy things but see me machining I was pretty lucky wasn't I? … I mean at work you were pretty lucky because if you went and bought a bit of material, I mean I could go down the Blue [the local high street]I mean the first suit I ever made was a three quarter jacket and a suit underneath I had a grey jacket and a blue skirt. It cost me one pound but then when you took it a work you know what you gonna have made out of it, you give the cutter one shilling he'd cut it out done it, and then you give one of the girls six-pence to under-press it and when you finished it give her six-pence and she'll top press it for you and you treat the girl to put some buttons on and you come home all dressed up made up to go out.[53]

Alice, using the machines and skills of her fellow workers, was able to get the outfit she wanted by appropriating work skills and time to have her own clothes made. Many girls knew that the way to obtain fashionable clothes was for them to make their own. Evidence would seem to indicate that teenage girls made instrumental use of the evening institutes that had been set up in the area. Numerous reports from the women's institutes and the girls' clubs show that enrolment in dressmaking classes was always relatively high. This was partly because they catered for the needs of those attending and as one report noted, staff understood their students and kept up with the modern fashions. Interestingly, this report also commented on the fact that there was only one machine on which pupils could sew their garments, so that much of the machining had to be done at home.[54] Despite the popularity of such classes, in 1928, the head teacher at Fair Street noted that the cost of materials was a factor that prohibited many girls from joining the classes.[55] The lack of machines did not deter girls from making their own clothes; it simply meant that they had to sew by hand, and if they could not afford patterns they became adept at making them up themselves, as Lucy described: 'I made me own clothes yeah ... 'cos I didn't have a sewing machine, I just made the pattern up meself ... that's how it was.'[56] One of the strategies that girls drew upon was the long-standing system in working-class neighbourhoods of buying things on 'tick',[57] which had arisen due to the irregular patterns of income that they experienced. In order to survive economically, it was quite common practice for those living in poor neighbourhoods to adopt a system of buying essential things like food on credit when they were hard up – which was often on a regular basis. 'There was only one shop near us – Aunt Lals we called it – and it sold sweets and groceries and things like that. You never paid for things with money during the week: they used to give you credit and you paid at the end of the week when the fathers got paid.'[58] Recalling this practice, women justify it retrospectively by the comment 'we was all the same', revealing the way in which normative behaviour was redefined to suit the purpose of those in the locality rather than conforming to the norms of those in wider society. This also reinforces the idea that culture is comprised of a system of meanings and values that are constantly being created in different social settings. In many ways, their use of buying on 'tick' was not unlike middle- and upper-class girls having an 'account' at a shop. The use of varied forms of credit became significant for girls' entré to commercial leisure as it enabled them to gain access to the fashionable styles of the day. This effectively made accessible a wider range of representations that they could draw upon to create a sense of identity and to stand out in some way. For those who could not make their own clothes, there was always the possibility of taking advantage of one of the many forms of informal loan clubs that operated in the neighbourhood. Such clubs were a well-established part of working-class culture, with some clubs specifically for particular goods or services, while others were more wide-ranging. What is evident is that, within working-class neighbourhoods, there was a thriving micro-economy in place that often provided the means by which groups maintained their respectability. In fact, Robert Roberts claimed that for many women a 'tick' book became a symbol of respectability as it acknowledged that they were trustworthy.[59] Some clubs operated among neighbours while others did so from the workplace, the exact nature of these clubs being varied. Girls also used their own initiative to set up their own clubs to save for stockings, scent or clothes at local shops, all essential prerequisites to enable them to rehearse their identity as a modern girl:

> I used to run a club for stockings and have me hair permed you know, about three-pence a week. Stockings was only one shillings and six-pence 'cos we couldn't afford it. So I run a club for the stockings. … I go round and collect the money when I collected one shilling and six-pence I'd go round there and she'd mark me card and I'd get a one shilling and six-pence pair of stockings. 'Cos they used to pick out of a hat you know. … Then I done the perms and one thing and another it wasn't a lot of money but you couldn't afford it all at once.[60]

These arrangements on the part of local shops to agree credit were condoned by shopkeepers who, as Hoggart has suggested, knew that the shop would not prosper without respecting the practices of the locality, thus demonstrating the power of local practices.[61] The use of clubs in this way signified the instrumental way in which collective responses were used to gain a sense of individuality via collaborating with other girls in terms of fashion. Although these clubs were common in working-class neighbourhoods, there was always a tension surrounding the need for everyone to keep up with their payments in order that the system worked. The Tallyman was also used as a means of buy now pay later:

> I had what we called a tally man, what you paid one shilling a week to buy your clothes. I was one of the smartest girls in Red Cross Street. As soon as I got near to paying up I used to say can I have something else? He used to bring a catalogue to our door, I used to say to him tell me when I have nearly paid up so that I can have some more new clothes.[62]

The need to be fashionable was often resolved through the sharing of clothes, which became an important way for the individual to be able to be dressed in what she considered an appropriate style. Again, it was a practice that was not new, and still continues. Margaret recalled that having handed over her wages of twelve shillings to her mother, she received two shillings back for her spends and had to consider wisely what was essential spending; for her it was having the right brand of stockings: 'I spent my money on Bemberg stockings … with the line up the back of the leg and I used to say to my sister "Have you got a good one so I won't have to buy any?" I had a good one, she had a good one, we had a pair'.[63]

The many magazines that were published at the time provided much of the stimulus for teenage girls to seek out the fashionable styles, and again, the sharing of resources came into play as the magazines were circulated within groups of friends. 'I bought magazines *Betty's Paper*, *Peg's Companion*, and *Red Letter*. Used to buy comics and swop 'em whatever ones your mate Ivy had, she changed with me for hers, that's how we used to get on.'[64] Some girls found more ingenious ways to get around the fact that they had limited money to purchase what was considered essential in order to achieve 'the look', and this was no more so than during the height of the craze for the Charleston when the right accessories were all important.

It had come out, the fashion, garters with bells, Charleston Bells on your garter, you could buy Charleston garters. I never had none but the babies had reigns you'd hold 'em up with and they used to have bells on, so I cut the bells off – there were always babies in our house. My father was at the gate where we lived and the girls from Atkinsons [a local perfume factory] used to come through there to work and as they went along you used to hear the bells ringing you know. My father was leaning on the gate, he said to my brother, 'What's all that?' and I was there 'Can you hear bells?' and my brother said 'Yeah dad, don't you know, that's the Charleston garters they got'. So my dad said 'Hope you don't wear them,' I said 'No I don't.' 'You liar you do' my brother said, he goes 'You know the bells on Maisie's reigns, she's cut 'em off'. I was about sixteen then.[65]

Clothes also act as a way of marking out individuality in that implicit in the idea of being fashionable is a sense of not only wearing the latest styles of the moment, but also dressing in such a way that is different to the majority of people. The quest to wear what others outside of their social class wore may have blurred class distinctions superficially, but the need to be fashionable raised its own issues. While the savings club was a mechanism by which girls could purchase the latest fashions so that they could stand out, the way the club operated could raise its own contradictions. Alice described one such club that was run by a neighbour. The money gathered enabled the holder of the money to buy clothes wholesale, but the problem was that the outfits purchased were all the same. Alice recalled: 'It used to be funny down Bevington Street. ... A woman used to let out money go over the warehouse and get things. You used to see them [girls] on a Saturday night they'd all go out in pairs all in the same clothes same dresses all dressed up alike.'[66] While adopting a collective response to their lack of funds to purchase the fashions they required, the intentions of working-class girls were not necessarily to seek a collective identity; what was more important was to publicly display the ability to wear something new. The

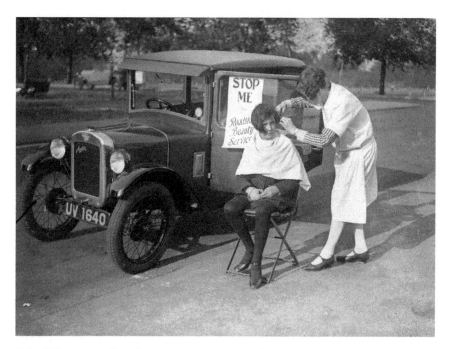

FIGURE 5 *Travelling hairdresser. Courtesy of Mary Evans Picture Library.*

current fashion mantra 'you are what you wear' was in evidence during this period. Peiss has suggested that dress was a way to assert an identity and some form of independence as well as social mobility.[67] In many respects, clothes symbolized the attempts on the part of girls to reproduce forms of identity that were perceived to be of their own making rather than adopting those already established for them. This is not dissimilar to the symbolic significance of the style of teenagers in the post-Second World War era. Often, the desire was to have something that was new and fashionable that allowed girls to perform a role that had little to do with the reality of their lives. Jerry White has confirmed the importance of clothes, arguing that they became a public obsession for women during this period as they symbolized independence.[68] The significance attached to clothes was not new. In 1911, Paterson commented on the amount of money that women in Bermondsey spent on clothes compared with the low levels of pay and relatively high prices. He suggested that the desire to spend money on clothes was due to personal vanity.[69] However, to make such analysis is to miss the symbolic meaning in the decisions made by the poor to spend money on what was visible. Enstad has reinforced the need to consider the symbolic significance of the meaning which individuals invested in clothes. She argued that for working-class women, the wearing of clothes which otherwise would have only been available to those from other social classes, signified a rejection of an ideology which excluded them from the label of 'a lady'. She went on to illustrate the ways in which consumer culture has been used to gain identity and dignity.[70] The symbolic meaning of their pursuit of fashionable styles usually associated with those outside of their social class is mindful of Fyvel's analysis of what the Teddy Boy style symbolized in the 1950s. He talked of their quest for social emancipation, for their place in what he termed 'the new classless culture'.[71] In the leisure pursuits of teenage girls during the interwar period, there is some similarity in that they too were seeking to remove themselves from a style associated with the working classes. Indeed, in 1936, Holtby pointed out that with 'the true democracy of the talkies, the two-penny fashion journal and inexpensive stores, it is possible for one fashion to affect a whole hemisphere with no distinction of class and little of pocket'.[72] It is true that the advent of commercial leisure meant that there was greater accessibility to a wider range of images associated with different social groups in different social milieu. A parallel can also be made with the meaning of youth styles in the latter part of the twentieth century. Cohen has argued that the style of the Mods and later the Skinheads symbolized a collective response on the part of young people to their position in society.[73] In the same way, the adopting of styles of those outside of their class group by teenage girls in the interwar years symbolized a response to their subordinate position in society.

Access to fashion and style was also a means to resist forms of identity associated with the older generation and this involved the adoption of the changing fashions for clothing and hairstyles that were liberating for women. The Marcel Wave and the bob that became fashionable meant freedom from long hair, and long hemlines gave way to shorter ones denoting a symbolic freedom of movement for women that reinforced the differences between the older and younger generations. The ways that many teenage girls copied the styles of their screen idols not only caused concern on the part of those outside of their class culture but also brought to the fore a generational conflict. This is reflected in the remarks of Kathy talking of the elderly ladies with whom she worked:

> I had a quiff anyway they thought – brazen hussy ... 'Kathleen you've got make-up on!' – they didn't call it make-up – 'you've got powder on haven't you?' 'No, I have not,' 'Yes you have, you don't want none of that now. How old are you, fourteen? A saucy girl are you?' And Miss Wates used to say 'Do ye hair properly, look at you.' 'Why?' 'I can write a note to your mother about you.'[74]

This generational conflict centred around the use of leisure was to be found in different areas of the country.[75] In many respects, it symbolized the attempts on the part of youth to reproduce forms of identity which were perceived to be of their own making rather than adopting those already established for them. Teenage girls during the interwar period adapted images they had taken from the cinema, magazines and advertising hoardings to symbolize a rejection of the lifestyle of their parents and others in positions of authority. By interpreting cultural processes in this way, they were able to deal with the contradictions that confronted them in terms of models of being a girl, and the styles that they adopted were often an attempt at a total transformation of identity. Consequently, the gaining and maintaining of the attributes of style became for many a crucial aspect of leisure time. It was the attempts to keep up with fashions and style that were seen as problematic on the part of those providing leisure other than that of a commercial nature. Make-up was increasingly becoming accessible, and though girls may not have been able to afford the named brands to be found in the West End stores, they could buy cheaper versions from Woolworths and other local stores. Mary recalled asking her younger brother 'to go up the top and get me a box of Chamois Leathers and face power'. She instructed him that 'if they ain't got Chamois Leather get Phul-nana'.[76] Phul-nana cost as little as two pence.[77] The use of make-up by teenage girls became a subject of much controversy during the period and the wearing of lipstick in particular seemed to epitomize all that was wrong with wearing make-up. During an interview with a representative of the Press Association after having opened a Palace of Beauty in Bayswater, Jessie Mathews (a famous actress of the day) commented: 'London girls are too fond of applying the lipstick and there seems to be a new rage to paint their faces in colours which to my mind are simply ghastly. They vary between a sickly white and a deep orange. ...There is plenty of time to decorate after one has reached the mature age of thirty.'[78]

In 1932, a court case in London sparked a rather delicate discussion in the press about the North–South divide in relation to make-up. An article had appeared in the *Lancashire Evening Post* entitled 'Are Lancashire Girls Dowdy?' The article raised the question of whether London girls used more face powder than Lancashire girls. The question arose as a result of a recent court case in London when a wholesale firm of complexion powder manufacturers sued four Lancashire hairdressers for money due on face powder supplies. A witness had stated that Lancashire girls used less face powder than London girls and this assertion was taken up by a reporter who set out to find the views of Lancashire girls while being careful to target a cross section of girls working in different settings. The manageress of a beauty parlour in Manchester said: 'I think the witness was right. ...The girls here do not appreciate how much the proper use of powder can improve the appearance.' A typist in a Manchester city office when asked what she thought replied, 'Yes indeed. ...London girls use more powder than we do.

They make up and smoke terribly. I have seen them with their white noses and red cheeks, and I know. We in Lancashire aren't like that thank goodness I use only a little powder, and certainly no lipstick.' A Londoner visiting Manchester was asked her views: 'I've been in London for some time … and there is no doubt that London girls use far more powder than Lancashire girls. Here in Lancashire the girls seem dowdy and shabby. They don't seem to trouble much about their appearance at all. The London girls use more cosmetics but at least they look chic.' A shop assistant in Manchester said: 'I don't like the way the London girls make up. There is too much of it. … They should try to be a bit more natural.'[79] What is in no doubt here is that the style and persona adopted by teenage girls certainly did provoke strong views across the country and it is also a reflection of the girl asserting herself. The debate about make-up transcended social class. Another article in the *Gloucester Citizen* in 1932 drew attention to the reaction on the part of the Bank of England to the wearing of make-up by girl clerks. The article reported:

In banks and offices word is going round among the girl employees that the excessive use of lipstick, powder-puff and rouge is not considered to be 'the thing' by the powers that be. A notice has been posted up in the Bank of England in rooms where girl clerks work warning them that they achieved their permanent status in the Bank of England by signing a book in which they undertook to wear only dark-coloured dresses and to carry themselves with decorum wherever they went. The notice finishes by pointing out that the use of lipstick is a breach of this undertaking. 'Of course it is silly,' said Miss Kettle, Secretary of the Association of Women Clerks and Secretaries, to a reporter yesterday. 'Some of the girls threaten to use more lipstick than ever, and others who have never used it say they will buy some. One cannot stop girls wearing lipstick.'[80]

The message was clear that girls would present themselves in the way that they wished to be seen. The public debate about the use of make-up was also a source of concern within the Girls' Club movement. An article entitled 'The Modern Girl' in *The Girls' Friendly Society Workers' Journal* in 1935 noted, 'The modern girl is well groomed has an eye for colour and takes pride in her appearance. We older ones may not approve of her painted lips and finger nails; but she will get over this phase.'[81] Reflecting upon the girls who attended the girls' club run by the Cambridge University Mission, Miss Gill in her report to the Annual General Meeting of the Cambridge University Mission in 1928 stated: 'Some might describe the girls as travesties of girlhood. They came at first with powder and paint on their faces, but in a little time, a great change was noticed, the powder and paint were washed off and the girls looked quite nice.'[82] Such comments reveal the tensions in different understandings of what it meant to be a woman. The apprehension on the part of social commentators about the images that girls made use of to rehearse their identity, as well as the products that they consumed in terms of fashion, hairstyles and make-up, was not shared by girls for whom the images and products they drew upon had a very different meaning. Producers of commercial leisure like any other product wanted to sell their goods. The advertising of the latest fashions that abounded at the time fed the desire of teenage girls to copy the images they saw in the advertisements and was a mechanism by which capitalism successfully incorporated them into the cycle of conspicuous consumption – but it was on the girls' own terms. The purchase of clothes was more than just the act of purchasing, it had symbolic meaning; purchasing a fashionable dress gave girls self-respect and a sense of self-worth. While girls' eagerness to become part of consumer culture was seen as trivial and not a good use of their leisure time on the part of many social commentators, for girls this was far from the case as consumer culture offered them a new range of representations and spaces to explore identities. The industries producing the products that girls wanted to consume promoted consumption as liberating for women and indeed it was for working-class girls. As well as gaining pleasure acquiring the latest fashions, girls also enjoyed the escapism to be found in many of the stories in magazines. A popular theme centred on working-class girls who escaped from their class culture, often through marriage to the owner of the business they worked for; needless to say, they lived happily ever after. While this type of story might have been frowned upon by the middle classes for whom such stories might well be seen as giving teenage girls unrealistic expectations, for girls it was simply fiction – but there was always a suggestion that it could happen to them. Girls did not want to fit into a role that had been defined for them; they wanted ownership of who they were. Working-class girls often found ways to adapt the commodities available to them to serve their need to construct images of themselves and to appropriate forms of behaviour which had in the past only been available to other social groups. Ada recalled: 'My mother had a fur coat, as she got on better, you know, a black fur coat, and she didn't want it so me and my friend, we cut it up and made a shoulder fur, and we had big hats. ... Went to the cinema. We weren't half going to have a good time.'[83] It was not only fashionable styles of clothes that became an essential feature of looking the part; the wearing of make-up denoted style and the transforming effects of wearing make-up was an important facet of being well dressed and well groomed. It was a message that was consistently reinforced by the media so much so that make-up was much sought after despite its prohibitive cost. However, girls on slender means could be very resourceful:

At Christmas gypsies used to come round and sell paper flowers and my mother used to buy some and put in a vase, we never had a front room, so we had a big front room that went over the house they had my mum and dad's bedroom in there with an armchair like, and she put the flowers and the vase in there. As I run out of lipstick I found that dye come out of them, never had no lipstick so I used to take them stand in front of the mirror and put them on me lips. And one day sitting in there and my mum said to my brother 'Here Arfur' she said 'them flowers are getting smaller.' 'Yeh' he said. I never said nothing. My mate came round, said 'Got any lipstick?' I said 'No, I ain't got none but I said come upstairs, I do it with these' and we put them on our lips. My mum had forgot something; she come over and she caught us.'[84]

Religion was sometimes used by girls in an instrumental way to enhance their appearance, or as might be expressed today to 'accessorize' as the following account shows:

A girl told me one day that if you went along to the Priests' house in Tabard Street and recited the 'Hail Mary,' the Priests give you some beads to wear round your neck. So, although I was supposed to be a Protestant, I learned the Hail Mary, went along to the Priests' house and recited it and got the beads. That's why I can still say the Hail Mary today. ... It was bribery and corruption, really, but I didn't mind – I had the beads![85]

For girls growing up in working-class neighbourhoods, the renegotiation of a collective consciousness clearly became key to their quest to participate in the leisure pursuits of their choice, and as Peiss has suggested, cultural forms were not imposed on girls but were developed and articulated by girls themselves.[86] What is clear is that, during the interwar years, working-class girls were drawing upon the normative behaviour of their neighbourhood to gain access to the growing consumer culture that they wanted to be part of. Enstad has suggested that consumer culture offered working-class women who struggled with material and ideological constraints a new range of representations and symbols and space within which to create an identity.[87] When girls dressed in the latest fashions they were challenging the construct of the girl in the background that Montague was making reference to, thereby challenging the middle-class definitions of what it meant to be a girl. The smartness of girls setting off to work that observers commented on was essentially a statement about their dignity. Enstad has suggested that the wearing of smart clothes to work meant that girls could share and show off their clothes to one another, making dress a part of their workplace culture.[88] It is important to acknowledge the relationship between girls' working lives and their leisure activities as they were connected and sought to inform who the girl was. They could be workers, mother's helper within the home, pleasure seekers; all these forms of identity could fuse together to inform who the girl wished to be, reinforcing the notion that identity is not static. Girls' active use of the cultural products of the leisure industry shaped who they were and partly informed their subjectivities. This is important as subjectivity is about the process of becoming, which is never completed as the self is never fixed. It was in part the lack of understanding that the girl was always becoming someone that challenged those providing clubs for girls. Clothing became a visual signifier that pointed to who a person was; for girls who were poor the clothes they wore allowed them to become part of a more affluent world. For many girls, the ability to have access to new clothes once they began full-time work would have been symbolic as prior to starting work most of them would have had hand-me-down clothes of older siblings. New clothes and make-up made them feel glamorous.

6

Time, space and respectability

The young people of this new England do not play chorus in an opera in which their social superiors are the principals; they do not live vicariously, enjoy life second hand, by telling one another what a wonderful time the young Earl is having or how beautiful Lady May looked in her court dress; they get on with their own lives. If they must have heroes and heroines, they choose them themselves, from the ranks of film stars and sportsmen and the like.[1]

Priestly's observation catches the essence of the interwar years for young people. For them the world was changing, it was a time when they were no longer deferential to their elders or superiors without questioning why. They were able to choose from a wider range of role models to determine who they wanted to be and they had an expectation of time for leisure and, equally important, access to a wider range of leisure pursuits. It was this that impacted on perceptions of what constituted respectability across the social classes. For working-class girls, the new consumer culture offered a range of representations, activities and spaces with which to create identities. However, what it had to offer was not always approved of by the older generation. In 1932, like so many other girls across the country, Lil, aged fourteen and living in Bermondsey, left school on the Friday and started work the following Monday. At the end of her first week at work, in common with other girls she gave her wages, which were ten shillings, to her mother who kept 7s. 6d.; Lil had 2s. 6d. for spends. Lil recalled what she did with that money:

> One of the first things I did was to go to Woolworths and buy a pair of clip on earrings, crystal balls you know and as soon as I put them on my mother looked at me and said 'You're not going out like that, you don't know what you look like, you look like one of them'. Well I didn't know what one of them meant, but now I understand what she meant.[2]

Two years later in 1934, commenting on the 'girl,' Burke noted, 'The London girl is always of course under fire of criticism concerning her behaviour and her dress.'[3] Burke was certainly correct: the London girl was the subject of much criticism particularly in the context of her leisure pursuits. Like girls in other parts of the country, she was the subject of considerable scrutiny in the media, she was the focus of attention at conferences organized by a number of different groups who had an interest in the welfare of young people and, as the period progressed, policymakers were concerned about the development of young people into good citizens.[4] Two key questions arise from this: what was it about working-class girls' behaviour which aroused so much concern and why? The answers to these questions are to be found by exploring the ways in which their leisure pursuits unsettled the received hegemony and more specifically notions of respectability that were challenged and reordered during the interwar period. Lil's purchase of earrings with her first wages demonstrates the importance to teenage girls of looking stylish. It was part of the new femininity to which they could gain access. Her mother's comment – 'you look like one of them' – is imbued with symbolic meaning about status and maintaining a good reputation as well as an acknowledgement of the ramifications of a bad reputation. While it has been suggested that youth are always a vector of social change,[5] equally respectability is a useful barometer of social change in that the cultural signifiers of respectability shift as individuals seek to assert their place in the social order. What is of interest here is how girls' leisure activities symbolized a challenge to power relations throughout the period and disturbed notions of respectability. Whether they were consciously aware of it at the time, teenage working-class girls were challenging what constituted respectability through their use of leisure. It was their use of time and space in particular which unsettled conventional understandings of what constituted respectability and more specifically what it meant to be a respectable working-class girl. This scenario was played out on a number of different layers and levels in society and in many respects set the groundwork for the post-Second World War generation who also challenged the social mores of the time. Respectability is not simply something that is externally imposed; it also works within communities to set boundaries and expectations and is often defined and judged in relation to the 'other'. Given that what constituted respectability was defined both within and outside of working-class communities, inevitably its constituents would be based upon different criteria. Giles has suggested that respectability is often influenced by the socio-economic situation of a given time.[6] Certainly, there has been a tradition of categorizing the working classes based upon economic criteria. Booth, for example, during the late nineteenth century had subdivided the working class, distinguishing them in relation to those living in abject poverty and those living in relative prosperity.[7] Such divisions were reinforced by cultural and environmental factors enabling the 'rough' and the 'respectable' to be distinguished from one another. The distinction between 'rough' and 'respectable' remained a compelling perception during the interwar years, not only in the eyes of middle-class observers but also within the working classes themselves.[8] However, these distinctions are too simplistic, as communities were far more nuanced and fluid, comprising layers and levels of experience which influenced the individual's place in the pecking order as well as how the community as a whole was understood from the outside. Certainly, within working-class communities the subtleties of defining respectability were complex; as Tebbutt noted, 'What was "ordinary" behaviour in one area might be defined as "rough" in another area within the same community.'[9]

Physical space had long been a marker of respectability for all social classes and, as such, often formed the basis of assumptions about those inhabiting that space. For example, the street was a powerful space as it signified who the individual was in relation to others and, as a consequence, judgements about respectability were made based upon this. Booth was able to observe a demarcation occurring within Bermondsey with a better class of person in the parishes of St James, St Luke, St Anne and St Phillip; in fact, the parish of St Anne was described as the Belgravia of Bermondsey.[10] Such differences still existed by the interwar period, when the NSL noted that there was not a middle-class street in the whole of the borough of Bermondsey, although there was some better working-class housing in the area south of Southwark Park.[11] Distinctions like this were not particular to Bermondsey. Robert Roberts talked of streets having social ratings and there being a social pecking order in Salford.[12] The street had long played a pivotal role in the lives of the urban poor and, as such, had become the subject of much public commentary.[13] Meacham talked of the street being more than just a space in which people lived. He saw it as a social setting which had meaning for those within it and those outside of it.[14] Certainly, within working-class neighbourhoods, people created their own internal signifiers of respectability; those living in Bermondsey were quite aware of a pecking order, as Iris recalled: 'People who lived in Reverdy

Road were considered a more artisan and middle-class type. There were plenty of roads and streets in Bermondsey where labouring men lived that were considered select. ... No-one ever hung clothes out on a Sunday and no-one ever spoke to people at the front door. That would have been considered vulgar.'[15] The possessions owned were also a marker of respectability: 'If you had a rug down in your house you were well off ... we had a settee and people thought we were posh because we had a settee.'[16] While these signifiers of respectability were clear to those within the community, they were not perceived in the same way by observers outside of the community. Part of the problem was an absence of understanding of why the working classes seemed to live so much of their lives in public space. There was often a lack of awareness that for many people the street was, by necessity of their cramped living conditions, an extension of the home and as a consequence a social space where lives were lived in the public eye. A number of writers have rightly pointed to this fact.[17] Margaret explained the space she grew up in: 'We lived in a flat nine of us with one bedroom, yes boys over that side and girls over that side. My mum in the sitting room on a put-you-up.'[18] Margaret's experience was not unusual in working-class neighbourhoods, but those who were fortunate enough not to have to live in cramped conditions could not always comprehend why families continued to live like this, and this lack of empathy often had an impact when they made judgements about the lives of the poor. It was not only the lack of space within the home that necessitated using the street as a social space, but it was also a lack of physical space within the community. Jerry White has pointed out that in London the streets formed the largest open spaces.[19] Certainly in Bermondsey where there was much overcrowding there was only one park in the whole borough. For girls growing up during the interwar years, the idea of the street being an extension of the home was the norm in many working-class neighbourhoods. For them it was a place of socialization. A study carried out in 1933 by Bakke noted that the streets were used constantly, especially in the evenings and on Sundays and holidays, when girls would be walking along the street in twos and threes, maybe stopping to chat to boys.[20] Certainly, the teenage girl saw it as a site of social engagement: it was used to practise the latest dances and it became a meeting place. 'Most of our entertainment was where we lived when we were kids. Next door to us was a barber's shop and past that was blank wall. There was a bit of wide pavement there and that was where we practiced our dancing.'[21] Lil recalled: 'Don't know where I learnt to dance ... used to practice it sometimes of a night underneath the lamp where we lived nobody took no notice of you.'[22] The street was a dynamic place: it was a site at which opinions about the individual were formed and tensions between different groups were played out. For women in particular it was an important centre of social life; it was a space where they had a powerful influence. Tebbutt has suggested that the street was a 'moral arena'[23] and it was one where women played a pivotal role, adopting a more public persona than the privatized working-class male whose life revolved more around working outside of the immediate neighbourhood.[24] Much has been written about the impoverished living conditions of the working classes during this period and it has come to define them in terms of expectations of behaviour and lifestyle.[25] What is important to acknowledge is that the dynamics of communities are not static; by their nature they change over time, and are not stuck in stereotypical images that those on the outside often perceive. Jerry White has pointed out that change in communities is likely to be found in 'disunities' in the 'contradictions of social life' which impact on the community as much as those outside of it.[26] These tensions were not particular to England. Drawing upon research into the lifestyle of young working women in turn-of-the-century New York, Peiss has suggested that young people claimed ownership of the streets during this period.[27] These contradictions of social life were revealed as the new leisure culture enabled working-class girls to leave, albeit for a brief moment, the lifestyle of the community to which they belonged out of necessity rather than choice. This was partly responsible for the conflict about leisure pursuits between working-class girls and their elders both within and outside of the community.[28] It was the lack of understanding of the centrality of the street in their lives that came to symbolize what was deemed to be wrong with the leisure pursuits of teenage girls.[29] Throughout the period there is evidence from numerous organizations involved in providing leisure for teenage girls of ongoing concerns about how 'the girl' used the street as an integral part of her social life. What this does reveal is a limited perception of how and why public and private space was used by the working classes. Certainly, autobiographical sources show that the separation of a private–public space had little meaning.[30]

Ideologies of respectability emphasized a need for conformity in some way, but what constituted respectability was not fixed; it was far more fluid, its constituents being changeable according to the social context. Often, respectability was about adhering to a set of values devised by those outside of the culture of the individual. As a consequence, what constituted respectability was not always uniform across class cultures, but rather, operated in a disparate way as to denote a power relationship in which the working classes were seen as limited. It was partly this relationship that had historically prompted those working in the voluntary sector to perceive the club as the setting within which to 'socialize' working-class girls. Implicit in this was the assumption that working-class culture was somewhat lacking in terms of respectability and the club was the forum for girls to engage in activities that denoted codes of respectability and order. The Girls' Club movement was vocal about how the teenage working-class girl spent her leisure time throughout the period. When Rooff's survey of the range and quality of youth work in England was published, it was noted that it 'will be of great service to everyone concerned with the problem of girls and their leisure'.[31] Talking of the work that had taken place in the early days of clubs, she referred to it as 'social ambulance work'.[32] The term is interesting as it implies a sense of curing deficiencies in some way and indeed it could be argued that this was what some in the Girls' Club movement wished to do in terms of teenage girls' attitudes and behaviour. The language used to describe working-class girls by those outside of their class reinforced perceptions of them being unruly and lacking respectability. In many ways, it confirmed assumptions about working-class culture that perceived it to be potentially threatening to the prevailing social order. The labelling of girls according to a typology that described them as 'the factory girl' or a 'certain type of girl' permeated much of the debates about the lifestyle of working-class girls especially throughout the early part of the interwar period. Such images were confirmed by Rooff who commented on the need for more clubs in Bermondsey to cater for the 'rougher' type of girls who could not settle to any activity that required concentration.[33] The assumption underpinning such comments reinforced the idea that a greater intensity of input on the part of the Girls' Club movement would eventually re-socialize working-class girls into an image that was seen as respectable. Humphries has affirmed that the perception of working-class youth in public discourse was that they were unstable and unruly.[34] Certainly, this idea of instability comes across in many descriptions of working-class girls that refer to their lack of discipline. Frequently, reports from girls' club managers made reference to the 'rough' sort of girl who was 'rowdy and boisterous'. Reporting in the *Girls' Friendly Society Workers' Sub-Committee Journal* in 1924, it was noted that 'more and more we get in our club the "very rough" sort of girl who divided her evenings between the streets, the "pictures" and on occasions cheap dances'.[35] What such comments reveal is a lack of appreciation of why girls chose to spend their free time in this way. It was not just about how they spent their time but where they spent their time. The theme of using time in a seemingly unproductive way on the part of teenagers was also evident in a comment made by Harris in a study of the uses of leisure in Bethnal Green, an area in east London that had similar socio-economic conditions to those of Bermondsey. Talking of the boys and girls who had just left school and were seen to constitute a problem, Harris noted:

They have gained a certain amount of economic freedom, without knowledge of how to use such independence. Leaving school and plunging straight away into factory life with an 8 hour day or longer, they arrive back in Bethnal Green tired, often noisy, and undisciplined, a reaction from the pressure of their work. ... No form of mental effort, nothing savouring of school, will be tolerated, but something must be found which ministers to their love of colour, and movement, and excitement.[36]

What was seen as harmful and wrong in terms of the behaviour of young people was endorsed in a talk given by Mr R. Kennedy Cox of the Docklands Settlement in Bermondsey, entitled 'The Girl with the Limited Outlook'. He described this girl as 'rough' or 'tiresome'. She was a girl 'who hung about street corners and whistled at boys'.[37] The journals of the Girls' Club movement provide a rich source of evidence of the chasm in understanding of girls' lives on the part of some club workers. A recurrent theme was what constituted respectable spaces for girls, the street not being one of them. The concerns of Mr Kennedy Cox in 1922 about girls hanging around on the street were not new. Observing the ways of adolescents in London in 1911, Paterson said that London working-class adolescents had three real interests: smoking, clothes and conversation.[38] In 1938, misgivings about how time was spent were echoed by Durant who claimed that 'the girls' imaginations tend to centre around the three things which experience has taught them are valuable – money, frocks and boys'.[39] One of the central aims of providing clubs for teenage girls was to counteract the influence of what was perceived to be undesirable spaces such as the street, the cinema and the dance hall to name a few. Evidence from those who sought to provide leisure facilities for the working classes suggests that the street was seen as a site of illicit pleasure, one of danger and an undesirable place. This was reiterated in the log books of numerous education institutes such as the Cosway Street Women's Institute in the West End of London that ran a club for girls. The log book refers to the club being open for two hours each evening for the 'rough' type of girl with the specific objective of keeping them off the street.[40] It was not only the Girls' Club movement that expressed concerns throughout the period about the lifestyle of young people and in particular the use of certain spaces being dangerous in some way. A pamphlet issuing a warning from the National Vigilance Association against young people having time to get up to mischief, stated 'Do not make the mistake of thinking that it is always necessary to go to dance halls or cinemas to obtain pleasure; or to spend your time idling about the streets as so many girls do.'[41] In 1921, The Girls' Club Journal included a report on an address given by Miss Swayne of the Bermondsey Time and Talents Club about the psychology of the club girl. She reminded her audience: 'This girl ... lives always in a crowd. Privacy of the most ordinary kind is unknown to her. She has, as a consequence, to fight for her individuality.'[42] Equally, Dewar writing about the life of 'the girl' noted:

The streets to a majority of our people are their play-room and their reception room. That is to say, the streets to them are not merely passage-ways – connecting links between the place from which they set out to the place to which they arrive. Indeed this aspect is of very secondary importance. Yet 'the glamour' of the streets is curiously elusive and at no time of permanent duration ....[43]

Peiss suggested that the street was a 'multi-layered world' that provided for different amusements.[44] The front of the house was often used as a viewing area when there was an expectation of entertainment provided by neighbours. Mary, who grew up in Bermondsey, recalled: 'If it was a Saturday night we'd be sitting there and one of us would say I hope there's a fight tonight and there would be, they would come out the pub singing and fighting and rowing.'[45] The idea that such communities were insular and inward-looking with low spatial mobility was challenged in the interwar years by teenage girls gaining employment outside of the area, which provided them with an opportunity to broaden their horizons and to experience how other people lived their lives. Oral testimony from women who grew up in Bermondsey draws attention to the friendships they made with girls they worked with who came from other areas of London. As a consequence, it became the norm for girls to travel to other areas of London to socialize. The ability to work outside the locality not only provided girls with the means to broaden their horizons both mentally and physically, but also impacted on their perception of where they lived. Gladys, who was born in Bermondsey in 1917, worked as a dressmaker in the West End of London as a teenage girl. Naturally, she was always well dressed when she went out. She recalled going dancing: 'Sometimes we'd go to dances in the Rotherhithe Town Hall, but not very often because – don't think me funny – but they used to be a bit rough in them days. With us being dress-makers we used to think we was a bit. ... I s'pose you might say a cut above that sort of thing.'[46] It was also the case that girls in areas like Bermondsey took up a wide range of leisure pursuits during the period which provided them with the opportunity to experience life outside of their neighbourhood. The popularity of cycling during the period gave girls the opportunity to literally see how other people lived. Lil recalled the places she visited when she was a member of the Bermondsey Wheelers Cycling Club. 'Every week I was off on a tandem, during the week you'd go up to the bank at Sidcup 'cos you could sit up on the grass, or the pond just beyond Bromley – Keston Lake, that was another one, Windsor.'[47]

Richards has suggested that by the interwar years new cultures of consumption and leisure were drawing young people away from the scrutiny of families and neighbourhoods and allowing them much more freedom.[48] This did indeed occur both physically and metaphorically as teenage girls had more freedom than their parents and more leisure opportunities and, as Peiss has suggested, they had access to newer forms of social life in the public arena.[49] Ironically, despite its popularity, the cinema was probably viewed as the biggest danger to the moral welfare of teenage girls. As girls were making optimal use of their leisure time with great enthusiasm, often attending the cinema frequently, this aspect of commercial leisure attracted vociferous concern in terms of its influence on the lifestyle of young people.[50] The supposed corrupting influence of it was seen as all-pervasive and was a consistent theme throughout the period within a wide range of organizations. Religious groups were interested in the moral and cultural impact of the cinema; the Public Morality Council, an interdenominational body that had been formed in 1899 to combat vice and indecency in London, had a designated cinema worker. The Christian Cinema Council had as its aim the promotion of 'the practical use and development of the cinema in the cause of religion, education recreation and social welfare'.[51] The minutes of local and national meetings of the organizations that provided clubs for girls and articles from their journals reiterate how acute concerns were about the cinema. At the Girls' Friendly Society meetings there was discussion in early 1923 about the merits of cinema going and whether it was a danger spiritually.[52] *The Girls' Club Journal* commented: 'The cinema is probably the chief source of an evening's amusement at the present time, and the cinema is probably the worst form of entertainment which exists to-day. The majority of films show pictures which deal with the more sordid forms of life, low crime and sensational murder, unhappy homes and lives, unfaithfulness of husbands and wives ....'[53] Twelve years later, the same theme was still resonating. An article entitled 'The Effect of the Cinema on Girls Ambitions' in the society's *Journal for the Workers* claimed:

> In these modern days the cinema is for good or evil, one of the greatest influences in the lives of our young people. Much of their spare time is spent at the cinema, a good deal of their pocket money is expended on it, and it plays a large part in the forming of their ideas and their estimate of relative values. Most serious of all, their ambitions are, in many cases, shaped by it, and the summit of the ambition of a not inconsiderable section of the youth of today is to be a successful film star.[54]

An indication of the severity of the concern about the influence of the cinema was demonstrated by the findings of the National Council of Women's Cinema Committee which had between 1930 and 1931 carried out an enquiry among county boroughs and county councils in England and Wales to investigate the extent to which licensing regulations recommended by the Home Office had been adopted. A great diversity was found. They formed a joint committee with the Mothers Union and the Public Morality Council as well as some other associations to widen the enquiry to all local cinema licensing authorities individually. A speech given by Mrs Ogilvie Gordon summed up the conclusions drawn from the survey:

> We view with apprehension the influence of a number of the tendentious, unwholesome films on the susceptible minds of a large proportion of the young people who compose the majority of the film audiences. We submit that the cumulative effect of viewing week after week, themes of ungoverned human passion cannot but undermine and confuse the ideas of right and wrong, of the normal and abnormal, and lead to a craving for thrills in real life comparable to those on the screen.[55]

Indeed, such was the concern about the nature of films that girls were watching in 1935 that the Girls' Friendly Society began a monthly column recommending suitable films as well as a summary of those considered bad. *Goin' to Town*, an 'A' rated film starring Mae West, was not recommended; the comment about the film was, 'The name of the star will tell you all you want to know about this one, which is in no worse taste than her previous efforts.' The best film that month was the *Scarlet Pimpernel*.[56] It was not just the films that were seen as corrupting, but the whole ambience of the cinema. As early as 1917, *The Girls' Club Journal* contained an article advising club workers how to complain about films. In the information given, it prioritized looking for cleanliness of surroundings, lighting, as well as noting the conduct of the audience. In particular, it pointed to the need to ensure that all parts of the cinema could be seen at any time.[57] Both the environment of the cinema and the content of the films shown consistently came under their scrutiny throughout the interwar years. As well as anxieties about the extent to which girls absorbed the images they saw on the screen and developed a false sense of reality, there were concerns about the cinema as a physical space. It was often felt that girls were in some moral danger when they went to the cinema. It was noted in *The Girls' Friendly Society Magazine* that girls could expect to be chaperoned when they went to the cinema.[58] Mrs Arbuthnot, attending the Central Council of the Girls' Friendly Society, spoke of the dangers of girls going to the cinema alone.[59] Such sentiments about the influence of films were voiced with venom in the press in an article entitled 'East End Changes. What Mr. Charrington has Seen in 50 Years: Evils of the Cinema'. Mr Charrington, the writer of the article, had worked with the Tower Hamlets Mission for fifty years and said of the cinema: 'Today some of the cinemas which have taken their [music halls] place are infinitely worse than those old music halls, for not only are they hot beds for the spread of contagious diseases, but the immorality that sometimes goes on in the dark is too horrible for you to print.

It is the great evil of our times.'[60] The concerns voiced nationally about the dangers of the cinema in relation to youth would have resonated in most localities around the country. An article in *Cherio!*, the magazine of St James Parish Church Bermondsey, confirmed the widespread view that there was a need for guidance as far as cinema viewing was concerned. In the article, the vicar commented: 'Today everyone goes to the pictures, but many are getting bored with a diet of legs and lechery, the kind of film that advertises itself as "never were girls so luscious." So each month we will call attention to a few good films that are booked to appear in local cinemas.'[61] He advocated instead 'good wholesome entertainment' and provided an example of such a film, namely *The Unfinished Symphony*, about the life of Schubert. It is interesting that despite the passion in many of the entreaties about what occurred at the cinema, when numbers attending clubs began to fall and clubs workers were having to consider strategies to increase membership, the Southwark branch of the Girls' Friendly Society asked for permission to advertise the Girls' Friendly Society in the local cinema.[62]

Dominant discourses of respectability that were mediated via the middle-class philanthropic organizations were in fact imposing what Humphries claimed was a 'culture of deference'.[63] The outpouring of concerns about the behaviour and lifestyle of working-class girls on the part of the philanthropic organizations would seem to suggest that there was no parental guidance for girls in their home environment, but this was far from the truth. When Emmy changed jobs and started working at the Eldorado Ice Cream Company, her mother did not approve: 'I worked for the Eldorado Ice Cream Company ... my mum didn't like me working there she said it was too rough but I didn't notice it. Because I went home and swore one night, she said "You're coming out of there".'[64] There is much evidence to suggest that the quest for respectability was an integral feature within the working-class neighbourhood, but often the working classes reworked dominant norms of respectability to relate to their own priorities. For example, the nature of the concerns that parents expressed about the moral welfare of their daughters was not always imposed from above, but born out of a desire to break out of the poverty-imposed trap.[65] This was evident in the many rules laid down by parents which centred around monitoring where girls socialized and with whom. For example, some working-class parents believed that the cinema was an appropriate place for their daughters to go unchaperoned, unlike the dance hall that still had connotations of an environment where there was danger due to the greater opportunity for physical contact with the opposite sex during dancing. Giles has suggested that 'the cultural imperatives of respectability were a bastion against being labelled rough at such times of economic crisis' and a means of retaining self-respect.[66] This was evident in the regulation of their daughters in terms of what was acceptable behaviour. Like many women who were raised in working-class communities, when those who grew up in Bermondsey recall their teenage years they invariably remember the strict rules imposed by their parents – usually their father. Implicit in these rules was a keen desire for the family to be seen to be respectable by others within the community and there were particular signifiers that denoted respectability. Girls were allowed out during the evenings but there were strict rules concerning what time they had to be home; once they started work they were often allowed out until 10 pm. Many women recall the punishment they received if they arrived home late; getting a wallop or even being locked out of their home for the night was not uncommon, whatever the reason for their lateness. Clara recalled:

> We had to be in a certain time oh yeh eight or nine. Once you started work you stayed out till about ten. I remember one night I got a wallop 'cos I stayed out all night. Well I was working at the Brewery over at Wapping and a woman I met up there I made friends with and they used to go to a club over where she lived and it was too late for me to come home one night and I was frightened of walking through Rotherhithe tunnel.[67]

Even at an older age, girls were disciplined:

> As we got older I used to go dancing, Fox Trot, Charleston, Black bottom, Quick Step. We used to go to our clubs and that and as I say as we got older we used to go to a Dance Hall on Saturday night, the Flodden at Camberwell Green, Liberty Place, lovely memories of that place. You'd have two dances with them [boys] and then they was going to take you home but we couldn't stop out late, 11 o'clock Saturday night because we was going to that dance, half past nine, ten o'clock other nights. When I was late home I got a spank, I got many a spank for being late.[68]

Being home at a particular time ensured that the girl maintained a good reputation outside of the family but it was also thought to ensure her safety from the biggest fear and stigma: that of getting pregnant out of wedlock. While it was not uncommon to have children out of wedlock, the fear of unwanted pregnancy was ever present on the part of parents who recognized the economic consequences this would wreak on a fragile economic structure. The economic and social stigma of becoming pregnant out of wedlock made parents wary and concerned about the space their daughters inhabited. Lil recalled what her mother thought constituted dangerous places: 'I think it must have been my Methodist upbringing, you can't wear earrings and you can't go to dances. We wasn't really Methodist that's my way of explaining it you know, my mother had a thing about dances and the West-end these are things you don't do. I didn't go up to the West-end.'[69] Margaret also experienced the idea of some spaces being deemed as not suitable places to go to. She affirms this fear of boys on the part of her father: 'I wasn't allowed to go to dances dad wouldn't allow me in the dance halls. ... I don't know why. My cousin come down one evening and took me down ... near Dockhead Church where there was a dance hall. ... He [her father] found out. "Don't never go down places like that again." Scared the boys would get hold of me.'[70] For many teenage girls it was not only a case of being watched by parents, but also by elder brothers.

> My mum used to like to know where I was but I didn't always tell 'em. ... In the end me and my friend we used to get the bus to the Green Man Blackheath, I liked to get away off the manor 'cos I had brothers knocking about and ... if I was at a dance my Arthur would come out and ... if I keep on dancing with a chap he'd say 'excuse me' push the bloke one side.[71]

Ironically, in many cases the concerns expressed by working-class parents were not too dissimilar to those expressed by those outside the working class, an example of which was the attitudes to mixing with boys. Inherent in the concerns on the part of parents about where their daughters spent their leisure time was a fear of girls becoming too intimate with boys. Margaret's father was emphatic about this:

> During the week I used to go out and stand with the boys on the corner go for a walk and that, my mum didn't know. If I see me mum coming along I used to run. I wasn't allowed out with boys. ... I kept away from where my mum might see me. ... I was with a boy one night and my dad said 'was that you running along the road with a boy?' I said 'no'. 'I'm sure it was.' He said, 'If it was, you know what you'll get.'[72]

Throughout the interwar years, a crucial issue that taxed the middle-class philanthropists was whether they should encourage the mixing of the sexes in their clubs. As the period progressed, attitudes towards this relaxed somewhat within the context of ensuring an air of respectability was retained in terms of what young people could do at the club. As the expectation of time for leisure increased and leisure pursuits became more accessible to a broader cross section of society, it was discernable that for teenage girls some pursuits were seen as respectable and others not, reinforcing the suggestion made by Green, Hebron and Woodward that leisure is an arena where women are closely guarded.[73] The pub was often the source of generational tension as the evils of drink were well known in working-class communities. 'I certainly didn't go into pubs until the war started when I was in the ARP.[74] It wasn't the thing that young girls did – not nice girls. I don't know what a nice respectable girl should be doing but they weren't to go in pubs or dances.'[75]

Alcohol had for a long time been seen as a problem of the working classes in that hard-earned money was spent on drink to the detriment of the family. It was something that invoked rigorous campaigning by the Temperance movement, so much so, that in comparison, the cinema – often regarded as the modern demon – was seen as the lesser of two evils. Mr R. Kennedy Cox of the Docklands Settlement noted that while in the past a young man would take his girl to the pub and treat her to bottles of stout, now there was an alternative: the cinema. Although the physical atmosphere might be unhealthy, it was morally better.[76] What is interesting about this remark is the suggestion that the cinema was a qualitative improvement on the pub as a leisure venue. Yet the pub was often an integral part of the neighbourhood: it was not just a place to go to drink, it had multiple functions. Llewellyn Smith drew attention to the pub's centrality to the neighbourhood, in a similar vein to that of local shops providing 'tick'. The pub would often have numerous clubs running for men and women; they included holiday clubs and Christmas clubs, which enabled many poor families to save money to ensure that they were able to have some sort of celebration at Christmas. Some pubs allowed the Tallyman to ply his trade so that people knew where to find him. The pub was a source of news; collections were made for those who had died or fallen on hard times. Often, it was the place where people informally found job opportunities. It is interesting that Llewellyn Smith observed that it was easier to remain in a pub for a long time having only made a small order than it was in a tea-shop or restaurant.[77] Recognizing their role in the community and the fact that they were dependent for their livelihood on their customers, publicans often arranged day trips or Christmas parties for children. They also organized sporting events with other pubs, and for adults the annual 'beano' that comprised a day trip by coach to a seaside resort would have been arranged by the publican. While the pub was a central part of the neighbourhood, providing a space where individuals could meet socially, drinking alcohol nevertheless was not seen as a respectable pursuit, nor one that young girls should indulge in. For some, it was a vice that was to be avoided. When the Bishop of London was invited to Haberdashers' Aske's School in Acton to open the new library given by the school governors, the theme of his speech to the girls was alcohol:

It is the most mischievous thing in the world for boys and girls to take cocktails. Whenever you come to have a young man and he offers you a cocktail when he takes you out to dinner, don't go with him again – choose another.[78]

The idea that drinking cocktails suggested a lack of respectability was reiterated when Mrs Mary S. Cant, a former president of the Women's Free

Church Council, gave an address on leisure and amusements and firmly gave her views about alcohol: 'Don't think because you are being asked to have a cocktail you are being admitted to the smart set, it generally means instead you are being admitted to the low set.'[79] Another facet of modern life was smoking. Although smoking was not new, the idea of women smoking had long been frowned upon; it was perceived as an indication of loose morals and certainly not ladylike. This changed in the early part of the twentieth century alongside changes in the social and economic status of women and the ways in which the tobacco industry capitalized on this by promoting smoking as a symbol of female emancipation. In North America, the tobacco companies waged numerous advertising campaigns that focused on the emancipated woman's smoking of cigarettes and many of these campaigns were often endorsed by famous film stars. Smoking a cigarette was marketed as fashionable and stylish, personified by the image of the flapper with a cigarette. The cigarette became, in essence, a symbol of modernity. The advent of mass-produced cigarettes during the late nineteenth century meant that cigarettes were cheaper to purchase and the modern marketing methods appealed to the modern girl in terms of the messages the images of the smoker gave out. Although Tinkler has suggested that very few advertisements in magazines aimed at teenage girls featured women smoking,[80] girls would have seen the stars on the screen at the cinema smoking. Equally, many of the advertisements for cigarettes featuring images of the 'modern' girl would have been visible on the plethora of advertising billboards. The images of their heroines smoking would have reinforced what it meant to be the modern sophisticated girl who embraced the new femininity. In some respects, it might be suggested that smoking was repositioned as a respectable pursuit during the interwar period. Indeed, as early as 1919, the section 'Feminine Matters' in the staff magazine at Peek Frean commented on the way that most workers smoked as though this was natural and normal.[81] For some girls, smoking became another fashion accessory which enabled them to make a statement about who they were; however, for others, smoking gave out a less respectable image. 'I certainly didn't smoke, I don't think any of the girls that I wished to knock around with used to smoke either that wasn't very nice at all.'[82]

It was not just the older generation who made judgements about what constituted respectability; girls were making their own decisions, some of which were akin to the views of their parents. In answer to a question about whether she had ever gone dancing, Alice replied, 'No; who I went with was more on the select side.'[83] The idea that the teenage girl lacked any self-regulation was clearly not the case; rules about how she was expected to behave were deeply embedded in notions of respectability within working-class communities. Giles has suggested that 'working-class respectability was a complex cluster of values embracing female sexuality, material security, respect for authority and behaviour appropriate to this.'[84] It is rather ironic that the priorities of the working classes were not dissimilar to those of the middle classes, but what differed were the processes utilized to ensure respectability. For the working classes, clothes were undoubtedly an important symbol of affirmation of their ability to engage in the consumption of leisure. This became more accentuated for teenage girls who embraced the new femininity and affirmed what it meant to be respectable. The priority given to the importance of being able to outwardly take on the mantle of respectability was emphasized by the capacity to be able to acquire clothes, as Orwell, talking of the importance of clothes for teenage boys and girls, noted:

> The girl can look like a fashion plate at an ever lower price. You may have three half pence in your pocket and not a prospect in the world and only the corner of a leaky bedroom to go home to: but in your new clothes you can stand on the street corner, indulging in a private daydream of yourself as Clark Gable or Greta Garbo, which compensates you for a great deal.[85]

The care taken to preserve clothes once purchased reinforces the value placed upon looking smart that was equated with respectability. Jessie recalled her mother's ritual with clothes: 'What me mum used to do when she bought you something new you only wore it for best for the first year ... that is the way the clothes lasted.'[86] Style gave girls the means to be part of respectable society; being up to date with the fashions meant that they could metaphorically move away from their cramped living conditions and be someone else. They had their own ideas about what it meant to be respectable and this involved looking smart. Clothes were a powerful signifier and asserted the fact that girls were deciding upon their identity, and the clothes they wore allowed them to proclaim a sense of independence. While this was empowering for them in that it provided the appearance of upward mobility, their assertiveness unsettled notions of respectability. The importance of clothes was not just associated with the younger generation, they were also of symbolic importance for the older generation. Proper clothing in working-class culture had traditionally helped to define respectability. The weekly trip to the pawn shop to get clothes out enabled the wearing of 'Sunday best'. It was also an affirmation of needing to confirm a sense of respectability and social status, which was particularly so for men who liked to dress up and go out socially or at least have the opportunity to do so:

> I used to have to go up Laymans and get the things out of pawn Saturday evening ... 'cos my dad never knew my mum pawned, he'd have broke her neck I reckon ... she pawned my aunt's engagement ring and father's suit. I had to put all them all back you see; he went out Sunday, he used to dress up and go out.[87]

Pawning involved depositing goods at the pawnbrokers who provided cash for the goods, which could only be redeemed when the sum given by the pawnbroker plus the interest charged was paid. If the individual could not pay back the money, the goods were sold. Invariably, women would put things in pawn on Monday and take them out on Friday. By the interwar period, the younger generation of girls wanted the same opportunities to look smart and to be part of the wider cultural life.

It was not just the changing styles of clothes and leisure venues that gave girls the opportunity to think that their lives could be different from their mothers. During the interwar years, they were increasingly aware of social and political changes around them. Girls growing up in Bermondsey would have been influenced by the municipal civic pride that the local authority provided. Acute to the usefulness of tapping into the things that young people were interested in so that they could get their message across, the local authority took advantage of the novelty of the cinema in the 1920s to promote a healthy lifestyle. In 1923, Dr Connan, the medical officer of health in Bermondsey, decided to embrace the love of the cinema that many in the area had and to use it to promote an awareness of a healthy lifestyle and a sense of civic duty. Dr Connan devised what he considered humorous titles for the films such as *A Tale of Two Titties*, that was about ensuring babies had good quality milk, and another one entitled *Where There is Life There is Soap*. The short films he made aimed to attract an audience who may well have been rather apathetic towards his aims. Drawing upon different film genres, the humour and slapstick in his short films soon appealed to a wide audience as the red and yellow projector van with its slogan, 'Here comes good health', rolled into position on targeted streets where there were power plugs and open air films were shown to wide audiences. The project was successful in terms of reaching a large audience. In 1932, there were sixty-two open air showings of the health films with a total audience of 30,000.[88] These measures gave the local people a sense of self-respect by challenging the idea of the street as a dangerous space; instead, it was used in an educative sense, revealing the street as a place of pleasure rather than one of tension. Dances were regularly held at the town hall, and people were encouraged to go swimming and participate in other sports such as rambling and cycling. Crucially, what the local authority was doing in terms of its leisure provision was actively encouraging girls to take part in activities of their choosing.

Concerns about respectability come to the foreground at times when there are seen to be challenges to the dominant consensus about what the word denotes. Different groups have the capacity to rework what constitutes this concept. Superficially, it might seem that the various providers of leisure wanted to market notions of respectability in specific ways for teenage girls, but in reality they were in fact all actively reinforcing dominant ideological positions in terms of class and gender. This raises the issue that if leisure has the potential to reinforce dominant ideologies then it suggests that it also has the potential to resist ideological constructs. The concept of resistance is useful to draw upon when making sense of what the leisure activities of working-class girls meant to them and, equally important, what their activities signified to others. Wearing's suggestion that resistance can help individuals create new identities[89] is useful as it provides the scope to understand the significance of girls' leisure. The notion of resistance refers to issues of freedom of choice and individual empowerment;[90] in addition, the idea of resistance also raises questions about the potential for social and cultural change through challenges to existing power relations. Wearing's argument that women rely more on the sphere of consumption and leisure as a source of autonomy and a sense of individual identity was certainly evident in the interwar years.[91] Girls were doing this; the choices they made about how they used their leisure time were not merely about what sort of leisure to pursue but also about asserting their right to resist their ideological position in society and it was the commercial leisure sector that provided them with the means to do so. What this demonstrates is how leisure became a medium through which the contemporary shifts in social and cultural relationships were exposed. Consumer culture undeniably offered working-class girls an alternative range of representations, activities and spaces within which to create identities. Enstad's proposition that working women embraced the resources that the new consumer culture offered and shifted the cultural terrain to their interests is certainly evident in the priorities of teenage girls who embraced the new femininity of the period.[92] Girls were making their own choices about what leisure to take part in; they danced the dances they wanted to and not those like the Roger-de-Coverley which those outside of their social class often thought was a suitable dance to take part in. Some girls joined cycling clubs, some went rambling; the girls who worked at Peek Frean were allowed to join the shooting range and compete with the lads. Like those in other parts of the country, girls in Bermondsey were able to join staff sports clubs and compete against other local factories; they listened to the modern music of the day and frequently went to the cinema. By making their own choices, they were resisting those forms of leisure that reinforced submissive forms of femininity and their future role as homemaker and carer which was deemed an essential part of their subjectivity; indeed, the modern girl was presented as occupying space outside of the traditional feminine role.[93] It was this resistance on the part of girls that caused some organizations to reassess their policies and make compromises on some issues in order to attract girls back to the club. Examples of this were the gradual acceptance that they could not dissuade girls from going to the cinema and the acknowledgement that allowing boys to attend the girls' club on some evenings increased attendance. This does demonstrate a subtle shift in power on the part of girls who resisted what they did not want. By their actions, girls effectively forced those providing forms of leisure that were outdated to reconsider their provision in light of the competition from other forms of leisure. Girls were actively becoming consumers rather than producers.

The image of the factory girl that had come to symbolize what was wrong with the lifestyle of working-class girls still resonated to some extent during the early years of the interwar period and it influenced the ways in which they were perceived. Yet, the factory girl had changed. Jerry White has suggested that factory work gained a more respectable air by the interwar period.[94] Certainly, the factories were changing as the owners and managers developed a view that they should look after the welfare of their staff. Jerry White suggested that the factory was becoming a structural element of the new 'femininity'.[95] It became a resource to share ideas and start up clothing clubs to save collectively for the latest fashions or the latest hairstyles. Some factories recognized that the modern girl was a consumer and as such they catered for her needs. For example, a photo appeared in *The Daily Herald* showing a teenager wearing her work overalls and clearly at work having a manicure while some other girls stood around her observing what was happening. The photo was accompanied with the words 'Manicure for Girls', at a noted baked beans and tinned food factory at Harlesden near London.[96] Outside of the workplace, the girl was demonstrating a new self-confidence and independence by the clothes she wore. She was conscious of the need to be smart and stylish when out in public and what it meant to be stylish was confirmed in the magazines and adverts that she saw daily. The career girl and the emancipated woman were popular stereotypes of the time and working-class girls had the potential to gain access to some of the attributes of the emancipated woman. Access to fashion and style was also a means to resist forms of identity associated with an older generation. It manifested itself in the way that girls adopted the changing fashions for clothing and hairstyles which were liberating for women; by the mid-1920s, it was the fashion for hemlines to be above the knee, while hairstyles such as the Eton Crop and the bob became fashionable. Freedom from long hair and long hemlines denoted a symbolic freedom of movement for women that reinforced the differences between the older and younger generations. Making reference to the ways in which 'working-class fatalism and respect for tradition' were beginning to disintegrate during the interwar period, Tebbutt has suggested this was to be seen in the 'ambivalent relationships between older and younger women'.[97] Teenage girls also distanced themselves from their parents' generation in the ways that they used space. Davies has made the interesting observation that rather than have the doorstep as the focus of their social lives, they moved to the street corner.[98]

While the factory provided girls with space to create new identities, it also gave them a forum within which to resist authority. Humphries suggests that larking about was a way of resisting authority; it was part of their street culture.[99] Certainly, for some girls the factory often became the space for larking about as a response to attempts in the workplace to discipline them and the monotony of the Bedaux system of the production line. Larking about had been an issue for those running the earlier clubs for girls; ironically, having spent so much time persuading girls to join the clubs, club leaders had to throw them out. Humphries has suggested that their larking about was a response to youth clubs attempting to impose a civilizing influence upon working-class girls. He argues that they stressed control and cultivated deference[100] which many girls rejected as the period progressed. This resistance to accepting advice about how to behave properly was not new, as there had long been a suspicion on the part of the poor of the motives of those providing much-needed space to engage in leisure. This suspicion had been encapsulated some years earlier by Anna Martin who had been involved in the setting up of a lodge for working women in Bermondsey. Writing of her experiences, she stated: 'That a meeting of women should be held, primarily for the purposes of pleasure and recreation was something of an innovation in the district, and the women themselves were for a time suspicious and could hardly believe there was no danger of moral or religious lessons being slipped surreptitiously into the proceedings.'[101]

This wariness had come from what must have seemed to the women living in the area as a relentless stream of well-intentioned advisers who did not have a clue about the reality of the lives of the women they were advising. The leisure activities of teenage working-class girls provide evidence to suggest that many girls were rejecting leisure activities that taught them to be deferential and to know their place. Instead, they were drawn to the newer forms of commercial leisure, which empowered them to make use of their own cultural norms and practices to engage in leisure pursuits of their choice. Essentially, they created a space within which to actively determine the nature of leisure they would engage in. In so doing, they were able to participate in the activities that were accessible to other social classes, thereby rehearsing images they wished to create from models outside of their own culture. McRobbie has argued that aspects of consumer culture such as fashion can provide locations for developing positive identities.[102] Undeniably, space and place were important components in the construction of identity. The lives of girls growing up during the interwar years were different from their mothers' in that the variety of leisure pursuits available provided them with a means to construct their identities outside of the traditional role of wife and mother. Working-class girls were able to broaden their horizons both physically and metaphorically in order to draw upon a more diverse range of role models than those found in the local community. Green has drawn attention to the importance of leisure contexts as central to gendered identity construction.[103] While gender and class identities are constituted in relation to particular places and as such can be oppressive, girls had choice, they knew they did not have to have their mothers' lives and they were aware that they could form their identity from role models in ways that they wanted. For many girls, the films they saw at the cinema and the magazines they had access to provided them with the scope to indulge in the fantasy of the Hollywood movies.

Equally, for some girls the potential to have choice was demonstrated in their pursuit of the more long-established forms of leisure for girls. For them it had the capacity to offer some escape from their social surroundings as they conformed to what the club leaders desired. For some it involved dressing up to affirm a sense of belonging to groups such as the Girl Guides, which gave them access to experiences they would not otherwise have had. For them, this enabled a sense of belonging to groups outside of their own, thereby symbolizing respectability. Certainly girls had a confidence and expectation that they were going to have fun. But they were not just having fun: whether consciously or otherwise they were pushing the boundaries, asserting themselves and stating who they wanted to be. In doing so, they were resisting identities that others wanted to foist upon them. The point is that girls realized that they had a choice and as such created their own ideas of respectability, and this influenced their lives hereafter.

Afterword

When the girls came out to play they certainly made a stir. The ways that working-class girls engaged in leisure during the interwar years demonstrated that they were contesting subjectivities offered by dominant cultural forms in order to redefine ways of seeing themselves. What was significant was that they knew that they had a choice as to how to spend their leisure time. Their class culture was such that they found ways in which to gain access to leisure pursuits that the commercial sector had to offer by refiguring those practices that had long been part of the fabric of their lives. While using their creativity to gain access to the products of commercial leisure was not considered unusual on the part of others in their community, those who were not part of their class culture often disapproved of their behaviour.

The debates in the public domain that took place via the philanthropic organizations, concerned with ensuring that girls were engaging in what was considered appropriate leisure, reflect the fact that these organizations were sorely tested during the interwar years by many girls who were rejecting what they had to offer, or in subtle ways demanding a compromise as to what was offered by the organizations. While many of those involved in these organizations were reluctant to recognize that the world was changing, the more astute workers recognized the need for change. Throughout the period, the advice to club workers was invariably laced with comments about not appearing condescending to those attending the clubs and club workers were advised to persevere with girls they thought were a challenge. It was a difficult relationship as those responsible for developing policies about working with teenage working-class girls genuinely wanted to provide them with opportunities to broaden their horizons; however, the problem was that in some respects their ideas about who the girl should be did not fit with what modern girls wanted to be. After a long day in a factory or a workshop, girls wanted some light relief. Teenage girls could see opportunities in the dream landscape provided by the commercial leisure sector for them to escape the drudgery of their lives for a short time. With greater choice available, they made the most of the leisure pursuits that were available to them. When the girl started to assert herself, she became the subject of much speculation in the press; her persona was mulled over and views were offered about how she presented herself. The way she chose to spend her leisure time became the subject of much debate on the part of those who did not really understand what the lives of working-class girls were like. Although they were sometimes perceived to be frivolous, taking on an inappropriate persona in terms of their leisure pursuits, girls did in fact have harsh working lives. While they could move from one job to another with relative ease, they were, nevertheless, poorly paid and knew that they were not free from taking on chores in the home after they had finished working outside of the home. Leisure became a space within which they could assert themselves and make choices about who they wanted to be. What social commentators failed to realize is that that the girl was part of the production process that produced who the girl was supposed to be and she wanted to consume some of what she produced.

During the interwar years, leisure became a prominent issue. Not only was the nature of what constituted leisure the subject of debate, but crucially the question arose of how time for leisure was used. These concerns became part of public debate on both a national and local level, with strong opinion being voiced about how leisure was used in particular by teenage girls, who were perceived to be in need of guidance in relation to taking on their future role as wife and mother. This was to be found in the efforts of those trying to get girls to attend evening classes. Evidence reveals that some classes were more popular than others, the most popular classes being dressmaking.

The limited awareness of the nature of girls' lives on the part of some of those who were involved in organizing these classes was demonstrated in the lack of understanding that the nature of the work that girls were engaged in often prevented them from attending classes, rather than a lack of interest. This study has provided the opportunity to explore the impact of how the teenage girl was constructed during the interwar years. By focusing on a specific location, the ways that the day-to-day fabric of life enabled individuals to resist identities foisted upon them can be analysed. It allows for a more detailed consideration of the nuances of specific localities and can empower individuals in terms of how they perceive themselves. The socio-economic circumstances in a locality clearly have an impact on how individuals choose to use their time for leisure. The breadth of choice available to girls in relation to leisure during the interwar period reinforces the definitional ambiguities of what constitutes leisure and what it means for girls in terms of developing a sense of identity. Some girls were happy to spend their leisure time reading a book, others attended local clubs, others went dancing and to the cinema on a frequent basis. The point was that they had choice.

Focusing on a particular locality therefore has enabled these issues to be explored in the context of national debates as well as considering the implications for specific localities. This has been of value in a number of ways. It has provided the scope to explore how the day-to-day mechanisms of working-class culture enabled girls to gain access to leisure. It also offers a means to understanding how girls used their time for leisure. It has also demonstrated the need to challenge received wisdom about the structural features of work. For example, this study has drawn attention to the paradox that while the work that girls were engaged in was very often exploitive in that wages were low, the fact that many girls were paid at a piece rate meant that they were to some extent in control of how much they earned. For girls like Alice who worked in dressmaking or tailoring, they were able to take advantage of work in an instrumental way, knowing that the clothes they were making would soon be in the windows of the fashion houses in the West End.[1] Girls were perceptive and were aware of the world they inhabited; they noted the latest styles and used the skills they had learnt at work to make their own dresses and suits so that they were up to date with the fashions. Others who did not have these skills made good use of the many savings clubs available. They were, as Glucksmann has suggested, the consumers of the products they were actually producing, and as such the dynamic of power relations would seem to be being challenged.[2]

The interwar period was a time when the philanthropic sector had to reassess what its aims were and how these could be achieved. Many organizations had to revisit their original aims, make changes and move forward into roles that were new to them. Some organizations began to refocus their aims and to streamline their work towards an emphasis upon training for youth workers rather than being involved in 'social ambulance' work that they realized was outdated. These organizations were, in many respects, being challenged to rethink what leisure for girls should be in the modern world, and they had to realize the need to temper their expectations of what girls wanted in terms of time for leisure. The archives of these organizations provide much evidence of a changing awareness throughout the period of who the girl was and who she wanted to be. While she was rehearsing her identity, drawing from her heroines in the films she saw and the plush venues where she went to dance, those who organized what had been deemed rational recreation were coming to terms with a changing world that gave working-class girls greater opportunities for leisure. It is ironic that many of those who were involved in working with girls seemed to find it difficult to come to terms with the fact that the nature of leisure was changing in the modern world. Girls, however, embraced the modern world and were prepared to take what it had to offer.

It has been useful to explore the impact of national policies developed by organizations that worked with teenage girls in a specific location as it has provided the opportunity to consider the context of their impact. This is important as all communities have their own dynamic socially, economically and culturally that influence the impact of change. In this respect, this research has been important in terms of foregrounding the local dimension; for example, girls growing up in Bermondsey might not have been aware of the impact of the increased intervention by the local authority in the lives of those living in the area, but such interventions gave them a sense of freedom and self-respect. Importantly, this research has allowed for consideration of the extent to which economic factors intersect with opportunities for leisure. This study has shown that working-class girls were not just victims of their economic circumstances. Oral testimony has repeatedly revealed that girls could gain employment easily. Many girls enjoyed the brief moments when they could have a lark at work; they joined the savings clubs that were organized in the workplace and they used the machines and skills of those who worked alongside them to ensure that they were fashionably dressed when they went out in the evening.

Exploring how teenage girls made use of leisure has confirmed the ambiguities of defining leisure and reinforces the notion that it is something that can mean different things in different settings. It is therefore something that needs to be reworked in different contexts; for example, it is clearly different in terms of class and gender. The choices that girls made about how and where to engage in leisure were made in the context of what was available to them and what they wanted leisure to provide for them. For some girls, it provided the means to resist identities that were not of their choosing; for others it enabled them to engage in activities that those from other social classes pursued. The point was that girls were making choices and determining what they considered leisure to be and for them it was empowering. What has been revealed is the ways in which leisure came to be a defining feature of individual subjectivity.

During the interwar years, girls brought this to the foreground. While their wages might have offered them some access to leisure, they were clearly resourceful in that they drew upon their own class culture in creative ways that offered a sense of fun. Given the limited funds they had, this does suggest that access to what they saw as the right sort of leisure was a priority. When Iris spent all of her wages on a pair of gloves on the way home from work at the end of a week, her mother was no doubt displeased as the wages of teenage girls were crucial to the family budget. For Iris, the gloves were an important symbol of belonging to the new modern world and gave her a great deal of pleasure. While girls thought that they were simply finding ways to be part of the consumer leisure culture of the time, they were also challenging the ways that leisure had been conceptualized, revealing it to be a far more amorphous concept than the commonly held belief that leisure is simply juxtaposed to work. What this study has shown is the importance of valuing the day-to-day fabric of life as a mechanism for understanding why people engage in specific activities and what meaning those activities provides for them. It is clear that for working-class girls the interwar years were a period when they were able to rehearse their identity via their leisure pursuits. While they were engaging in the dream world of consumer leisure, they knew it was just fun, but it allowed them to escape, albeit for a short period of time, the drudgery of their lives.

Oral testimony has been valuable in this study as the recollections of the women reveal the eclectic range of activities that gave them pleasure. Although those outside of their social class might have considered them as outrageous in their behaviour in terms of wanting to have fun, they did have an awareness of the boundaries of their lives; they knew what rules needed to be obeyed like arriving home on time, but they also knew how to test the boundaries by having a lark. The women who shared their memories of growing up during the interwar years were keen to emphasize the importance of presenting oneself as a smart person and being able to take part in activities that others outside of their social class took part in. In doing so, they were confirming their right to take on identities of their choosing and resist identities foisted on them by others. They knew what it meant to be respectable. A major outcome of this study is confirmation that a teenage consumer culture was firmly in place during the interwar years. It was one that was dominated by working-class teenage girls who drew upon the creativity of their class culture to gain access to the leisure pursuits that others who had more disposable income were engaged in. The modern working-class girl was not going to be left behind; she knew that the strategies that had been drawn upon within her class culture over many years in order to survive could be utilized for what might seem to be frivolous means, namely participating in the new commercial leisure activities. What she did was adapt those practices to achieve her goal. However, her access to the leisure pursuits that those outside of her social class had access to had more than a frivolous meaning. She was asserting her right to participate in modern leisure activities and to be part of the modern world knowing that her class culture would provide her with the means to gain access.

What is significant is the evidence that girls were at the forefront of a teenage consumer culture during the interwar years, but this was for reasons other than levels of disposable income. This study has firmly established that working-class girls did not have to wait for a time when they might have access to disposable income in order to engage in the leisure of their choice; instead, they drew upon their cultural practices. It also confirms that girls were more than wives and mothers in the making. With the burgeoning of commercial leisure during the interwar years, they had a greater array of images of who they could be and to some extent the means to achieve it if only in terms of hairstyle and dress. Establishing that working-class girls were at the forefront of challenging roles that had been imposed upon them in relation to their leisure activities calls for a reassessment of the development of a teenage consumer culture. This study does nevertheless leave questions to be addressed. Was there a commonality of experience with girls in other parts of the country? Did girls in other parts of the country use similar strategies to gain access to leisure? What made girls get drawn into some activities rather than others? Was there a conscious or subliminal decision to be a particular sort of girl? These questions are suggestive of the need for future micro explorations of how girls engaged in leisure in different social settings and what for them leisure meant.

When girls asserted their right to participate in the modern leisure activities, their experience provided them with an awareness that their lives would be qualitatively different from those of their mothers. While girls' experiences as the modern girl were formative in terms of their identity, so too was the fact that they became the young women who experienced first-hand another world war. Living in Bermondsey, these women would have experienced the Blitz; some were evacuated and later returned, but many remained in the area for the duration of the war, being bombed out of their homes often more than once. After the Second World War, they would have taken on their roles as wives and mothers; most of them would have worked part-time, if not full-time, as the marriage bar was taken away in many companies. By the time their children reached their teenage years, style was changing for teenagers; it was the period of the Teddy Boy and Girl, rock and roll rather than the Charleston and the foxtrot, followed later by the arrival of the Mods and Rockers, again with their own styles of music and fashion, all of which signified the modern teenager. Their daughters became good examples of continuity in that they took on the mantle of the modern girl and reworked it. Subsequent generations have done the same thing. Girl power has become respectable.

Appendix:
Brief biographical
details of interviewees

Most of the interviews for this research took place at day-care centres in Bermondsey in the late 1990s.

Clara was born in Bermondsey in 1914 and was the youngest of four children. Her father was a lighterman and her mother worked at a local factory making the capsules for whisky bottles. Having left Cow Lane School at fourteen, she started work in a jelly factory. She later obtained work across the river at Wapping. Clara married at the age of twenty.

Lil was born in 1918 at Millstream Road near to Dockhead. She had one younger brother. Her father, who had been injured in the war, was a general labourer and her mother had been a print worker. Lil left school aged fourteen and had a brief period working at the Camberwell Beauty factory making jam pot covers. She then went to work in a leather factory. Early in her life she became active in politics and this took up much of her time. She married and continued to support political causes locally and on a wider scale. She remained in the same geographical area all of her life.

Iris was born in 1910 and was the youngest of fourteen children. She left Gallywall Road School at the age of fourteen and after having numerous jobs in local factories she decided to go into service at the age of nineteen. She eventually became a cook. Iris never married.

Sarah was born in Bethnal Green in 1914. She moved to Bermondsey at an early age. Sarah's father was a docker. Her first job was delivering papers. She later worked in numerous factories in Bermondsey.

Kathy was born in 1910 and had six siblings. Her father was a docker. Her first job at the age of fourteen was at a factory in Long Lane making ties. She later worked at the Alaska Fur factory. She married and had children and remained living in the area.

Jessie was born in 1918 and lived near Long Lane. Her father worked as a painter and decorator for the local council. Having left school at the age of fourteen, she went to work in the office at Spicers, a local paper factory. She stayed with the same company until she had her first son.

Alice was born in 1916 and was the eldest of three children. Her father was a lorry driver. Alice left school at the age of fourteen and began work training as a machinist and learnt the trade of tailoring. She made good use of her training throughout her life and remained in the area for many years.

Ivy was born in 1912 in Enid Street. She was the eldest of ten children. Her mother worked as a pram-upholsterer and her father was a carpenter. When she left school at the age of fourteen, she began work in Strakers, a stationers at Bishopsgate near to the City of London. She later worked in restaurants.

Margaret was born in 1918 at Dockhead. She was one of nine children. Her father was a docker. Her schooling was disrupted due to ill health. When she left school at the age of fourteen, she worked in a factory making tins. She married at the age of twenty-one.

Mary was born in 1907 and lived in an area of Bermondsey known as Downtown. She was one of ten children. Her father was a boat maker. When she left school at the age of fourteen, she began work in a local factory and stayed there until the age of twenty-four when her mother died.

Lucy was born in 1911 near the Rotherhithe Tunnel. She was the fourth eldest of twelve children. Her father was a docker and her mother worked at the local gas works. Lucy left school at the age of thirteen and began work locally at a leather factory. She subsequently worked in many factories in the area and was always in employment.

Emmy was born in 1911 and was one of eight children. Her father was a butcher, which meant that despite being poor the family ate well. She left school at the age of fourteen and began working in a print firm locally before going on to work in many of the factories in the area.

Lizzie was born in 1908 and was one of seven children. Having left school at the age of fourteen, she initially worked at a tailor's but then moved around finding work locally wherever the pay was the highest.

Lily was born in 1912 in Barkworth Road. She was one of ten children and her father was a manager at Peek Frean. When she left school at the age of fourteen, she had a job putting labels on suitcases. She stayed at this job until after she married at the age of thirty-two.

Maude was born in 1912 and she was the eldest in the family with two brothers and seven sisters. Her father was a carpenter. She started work in Strakers, a stationers in Bishopsgate north of the river Thames. She met and married her husband during the war.

Notes

Introduction

1 Stevenson, J. (1984), *British Society 1914–45*, Middlesex: Penguin Books, 246.

2 Ibid.

3 Osgerby, B. (1998), *Youth in Britain Since 1945*, Oxford: Blackwell, 6.

4 Fowler, D. (1995), *The First Teenagers: The Lifestyle of Young Wage-Earners in Inter-War Britain*, London: Woburn Press.

5 Bailey, P. (1989), 'The politics and poetics of modern British leisure: A late twentieth-century review', *Rethinking History* 2 (2): 131–75, 152.

6 Humphries, S. (1983), *Hooligans or Rebels? An Oral History of Working-Class Childhood and Youth 1889–1939*, Oxford: Blackwell, 1.

7 See, for example, Gillis, J. R. (1974), *Youth and History, Tradition and Change in European Age Relations 1770–Present*, New York: Academic Press; Hendrick, H. (1990), *Images of Youth: Age, Class, and the Male Youth Problem, 1880–1920*, Oxford: Clarendon Press; Davis, J. (1990), *Youth and the Condition of Britain: Images of Adolescent Conflict*, London: Athlone; Humphries, *Hooligans*.

8 Springhall, J. (1986), *Coming of Age: Adolescence in Britain 1860–1960*, Dublin: Gill and Macmillan, 5.

9 For example, Hendrick, *Images of Youth*; Springhall, *Coming of Age*; Gillis, *Youth and History*.

10 Springhall, *Coming of Age*; Hendrick, *Images of Youth*.

11 Dyhouse, C. (1981), *Girls Growing Up in Late Victorian and Edwardian England*, London: Routledge & Kegan Paul.

12 Hendrick, *Images of Youth*, 4.

13 Springhall, *Coming of Age*.

14 Humphries, *Hooligans*.

15 Springhall, *Coming of Age*, 120.

16 Parratt, C. M. (2001), *'More Than Mere Amusement' Working-Class Women's Leisure in England. 1750–1914*, Boston: Northeastern University Press; Tinkler, P. (1995), *Constructing Girlhood: Popular Magazines for Girls Growing Up in England 1920–1950*, London: Taylor & Francis; Enstad, N. (1999), *Ladies of Labor, Girls of Adventure: Working Women, Popular Culture, and Labor Politics at the Turn of the Twentieth Century*, New York: Columbia University Press.

17 Bailey, 'The politics', 152.

18 Ibid.

19 See, for example, Davies, A. (1992), *Leisure, Gender and Poverty: Working-Class Culture, in Salford and Manchester, 1900–1939*, Buckingham: Open University Press; Humphries, *Hooligans*; Fowler, *The First Teenagers*.

20 Fowler, *The First Teenagers*, 2.

21 Abrams, M. (1959), *The Teenage Consumer: Teenage Consumer Spending in 1959 Part II*, London: London Press Exchange, 3.

22 Davies, *Leisure, Gender*, 83–96; Langhamer, C. (2000), *Women's Leisure in England 1920–1960*, Manchester: Manchester University Press, Chap. 3; Alexander, S. (1994), 'Becoming a woman in London in the 1920s and 1930s', in Alexander, S., *Becoming a Woman and Other Essays in 19th and 20th Century Feminist History*, London: Virago, 203–24.

23 Giles, J. (1995), *Women Identity and Private Life in Britain, 1900–50*, Basingstoke: Macmillan Press, 2.

24 Dyhouse, *Girls Growing*, 116.

25 Abrams, L. (2010), *Oral History Theory*, Oxford: Routledge, 79.

26 Borland, K. (1991), '"That's not what I said": Interpretative conflict in oral narrative research', in Gluck, S. B. and Patai, D., eds, *Women's Words: The Feminist Practice of Oral History*, London: Routledge, 63–75.

27 See, for example, Walton, J. K. and Walvin, J. (1983), *Leisure in Britain 1780–1939*, Manchester: Manchester University Press; Davies, *Leisure, Gender*; Jones, S. G. (1986), *Workers at Play: A Social and Economic History of Leisure*, London: Routledge & Kegan Paul.

28 Jones, *Workers at Play*.

29 Walton and Walvin, *Leisure in Britain*, 3.

Chapter 1

1 Priestley, J. B. (1940), *English Journey*, London: William Heinemann Ltd and Victor Gollancz Ltd, 397.

2 Priestley, *English Journey*, 401.

3 See, for example, Greenwood, W. (1933), *Love on the Dole. A Tale of the Two Cities*, London: Jonathan Cape; Orwell, G. (1937), *The Road to Wigan Pier*, London: Victor Gollancz; Wilkinson, E. (1939), *The Town that was Murdered: The Life-Story of Jarrow*, London: Victor Gollancz.

4 Croucher, R. (1987), *We Refuse to Starve in Silence: A History of the National Unemployed Workers' Movement, 1920–46*, London: Laurence-Wishart, 15; Bourke, J. (1994), *Working-Class Cultures in Britain 1890–1960: Gender, Class and Ethnicity*, London: Routledge, 111.

5 Beveridge, W. H. (1930), *Unemployment: A Problem of Industry*, 2nd edn, London: Longmans, 406.

6 Bourke, *Working-Class*, 109.

7 Stevenson, *British Society*, 103; Beddoe, D. (1989), *Back to Home and Duty: Women Between the Wars 1918–1939*, London: Pandora, 54.

8 Stevenson, *British Society*, 114.

9 Ibid., 113.

10 See, for example, Beddoe, *Back to Home*, 67–70; Glucksmann, M. (1990), *Women Assemble: Women Workers and the New Industries in Inter-War Britain*, London: Routledge; Priestley, *English Journey*; and Roberts, R. (1973), *The Classic Slum: Salford Life in the First Quarter of the Century*, Harmsworth: Penguin.

11 Beddoe, *Back to Home*, 2.

12 Tebbutt, M. (2012), *Being Boys: Youth, Leisure and Identity in the Inter-War Years*, Manchester: Manchester University Press, 5.

13 See, for example, Alexander, S. (Autumn 2007), 'A new civilization? London surveyed 1928–1940s', *History Workshop Journal* 64, 290–6, 304–7.

14 White, *The Worst Street*.

15 See, for example, Tout, H. (1938), *The Standard of Living in Bristol*, Bristol: Arrowsmith; Llewellyn Smith, H., ed. (1935), *The New Survey of London Life and Labour*, London: P. S. King & Son, 3; Rowntree, B. S. (1941), *Poverty and Progress: A Second Social Survey of York*, London: Longman.

16 Llewellyn Smith, *New Survey*, 3, 134.

17 Ibid.

18 Ibid., 218.

19 *London Evening Standard* (27 January 1937), cited in Hutt, A. (1933), *The Condition of the Working-Class in Britain*, London: M. Lawrence Ltd, 127.

20 Llewellyn Smith, *New Survey*, 3, 78–96; Tout, *Standard of Living*, 21.

21 *Bermondsey Labour Magazine* (April 1920), 1, series 1.

22 Booth, C. (1902), *Life and Labour of the People in London*, 3rd Series: Religious Influences, 4. London: Macmillan & Co., 101.

23 Llewellyn Smith, *New Survey*, 2, 358.

24 Mary Mcquillan in Fagan, S. (1997), *Born in Bermondsey*, London: (s. l), 36.

25 Clara.

26 Llewellyn Smith, *New Survey*, 1, 31.

27 Lil.

28 Lil.

29 Davies, *Leisure, Gender*.

30 Llewellyn Smith, *New Survey*, 9, 417–25.

31 See Langhamer, *Women's Leisure*.

32 Beatrice Holder.

33 Devereux, W. A. (1982), *Adult Education in Inner London 1870–1980*, London: Shepheard-Walwyn, 115.

34 Lindsay, K. (1926), *Social Progress and Educational Waste: Being a Study of the 'Free-Place' and Scholarship System etc.*, London: G. Routledge & Sons, 87.

35 *Christchurch Messenger* (May 1933).

36 Borough Polytechnic Trade School for Girls Curriculum (10 April 1934).

37 'Socialists Build a Hundred and Fifty Thousand Pound Palace of Baths' (1927), *Daily Mirror*. Cited in Leff, V. and Blunden, C. H. (1900–65), *Riverside Story: The Story of Bermondsey and Its People*, produced and published by Civic Publicity Services Ltd, 34.

38 Lil.

39 *Bermondsey Labour Magazine* (November 1925), 23, 5.

40 *Bermondsey Labour Magazine* (June 1924), 9, 4.

41 *Bermondsey Labour Magazine* (September 1924), 11, 7.

42 Ibid., 5.

43 Ibid., 3.

44 *Bermondsey Labour Magazine* (June 1924), 9, 4–5.

45 *Bermondsey Labour Magazine* (September 1924), 11, 7.

46 Leff and Blunden, *Riverside*, 48.

47 *Bermondsey Labour Magazine* (July 1927), 42, 3.

48 'South London Women Workers, Fourteen Thousand Idle' (1911), *The Times* (15 August), 8.

49 Lil.

50 Rooff, M. (1935), *Youth and Leisure. A Survey of Girls' Organisations in England and Wales*, Edinburgh: Constable, 3.

51 Ibid.

52 Llewellyn Smith, *New Survey*, 9, 224.

53 Ibid., 224.

54 *Rules and Regulations of the Mission*, Cambridge University Mission Committee Meeting (10 February 1922).

55 Bermondsey Settlement Annual Report (1892–1901).

56 Minutes of the Cambridge University Mission (1 May 1931).

57 Address given by Reverend E. A. B. Royds MA at the Annual General Meeting of the Cambridge University Mission (15 April 1926).

58 Llewellyn Smith, *New Survey*, 9, 195.

59 Ibid., 4.

60 Ibid., 9, 1.

Chapter 2

1 See, for example, Abenstern, M. (1986), 'Expression and Control: A Case Study of Working-Class Leisure and Gender 1918–1939, A Case Study of Rochdale Using Oral Evidence', PhD thesis, Essex University; Langhamer, C. (1996), 'Women and Leisure in Manchester, 1920–c. 1960', PhD thesis, University of Central Lancashire; Tinkler, *Constructing Girlhood*.

2 Llewellyn Smith, *New Survey*, 9, 44–5.

3 Ibid., 46.

4 Jones, D. C., ed. (1934), *The Social Survey of Merseyside*, Liverpool: University Press, 3, 279.

5 See, for example, Deem, R. (1986), *All Work and No Play? The Sociology of Leisure*, Milton Keynes: Open University Press.

6 Jones, *Workers at Play*, 4.

7 Clarke, J. and Critcher, C. (1985), *The Devil Makes Work: Leisure in Capitalist Britain*, Basingstoke: Macmillan, 70–8.

8 Llewellyn Smith, *New Survey*, 9, 1.

9 Clarke and Critcher, *The Devil*, 3.

10 Ibid., 3.

11 Howkins, A. and Lowerson, J. (1979), *Trends in Leisure 1919–1939, A Review for the Joint Panel on Leisure & Recreation Research*, London: The Sports Council and Social Science Research Council, 1.

12 Davies, *Leisure, Gender*, 55.

13 Roberts, E. (1984), *A Woman's Place: An Oral History of Working-Class Women 1890–1940*, Oxford: Blackwell, 203.

14 Spring Rice, M. (1939), *Working-Class Wives: Their Health and Conditions*, Middlesex: Pelican.

15 Llewellyn Smith, *New Survey*, 9, 414–31.

16 Bailey, *The Politics*, 151; Green, E., Hebron, S. and Woodward, D. (1990), *Women's Leisure. What Leisure?* Basingstoke: Macmillan, 473.

17 Langhamer, *Women's Leisure*, 15.

18 Hill, J. (2002), *Sport, Leisure & Culture in Twentieth Century Britain*, Basingstoke: Palgrave, 2.

19 For example, Deem, *All Work*, 80–97.

20 Wearing, B. (1998), *Leisure and Feminist Theory*, London: Sage, x.

21 Wearing provides an excellent overview of late-twentieth-century feminist perspectives concerning women's experience of leisure. Wearing, *Leisure and Feminist Theory*.

22 Wimbush, E. and Talbot, M., eds (1988), *Relative Freedoms: Women and Leisure*, Milton Keynes: Open University Press, xiv–xxi.

23 Wearing, B. and Wearing, S. L. (1988), '"All in a days leisure": Gender and the concept of leisure', *Leisure Studies*, 7, 111–23.

24 Wearing, *Leisure*, 149.

25 Bailey, *The Politics*, 150.

26 Langhamer, *Women's Leisure*, 20.

27 Spring Rice, *Working-Wives*.

28 Wearing, *Leisure*, 145.

29 Ibid., 146.

30 Green et al., *Women's Leisure, What Leisure?*, 3.

31 Wimbush and Talbot, *Relative Freedoms*; Dixey, R. (1988), '"Eyes down": A study of Bingo', in Wimbush and Talbot, *Relative Freedoms*, 96.

32 Henderson (1996), 139.

33 Green et al., *Women's Leisure, What Leisure?* 6.

34 Spring Rice, *Working-Class Wives*, 99.

35 Ibid.

36 Ibid.

37 Langhamer, *Women's Leisure*, Chap. 2.

38 Tinkler, *Cause for Concern*, 234.

39 Tinkler, *Cause for Concern*.

40 *The Leisure of the People: A Handbook being The Report of the National Conference held at Manchester* (November 1919), 45.

41 'The Bournville Annual' (June 1926), in *The Girls' Friendly Society Journal*, 93.

42 Clarke and Critcher, *The Devil*, 64.

43 Giles, *Women, Identity*, 6.

44 White, *The Worst Street*, 161.

45 Parratt, *More Than Mere Amusement*, 5.

46 Ibid.

47 'New Generation that Lacks Sense of Responsibility, Maintaining Present Standards' (1935), *The Manchester Guardian* (20 February), 2.

48 See, for example, Burns, C. D. (1932), *Leisure in the Modern World*, London: Allen & Unwin; Durant, H. W. (1938), *The Problem of Leisure*, London: Routledge & Sons.

49 Tinkler, *Cause for Concern*, 235.

50 *The Girls' Club Journal* (October 1932), 8.

51 Tinkler, *Cause for Concern*, 234.

52 See, for example, Cutten, G. B. (1926), *The Threat of Leisure*, New Haven: Yale University Press, 96; Burns, *Leisure in the Modern World*.

53 Work of Men's Institutes in London (1926), The Board of Education, Pamphlet No 48, London: HMSO, 5.

54 Devereux, *Adult Education*, 70.

55 Llewellyn Smith, *New Survey*, 1, 50.

56 Ibid., 4.

57 See, for example, the Log Book of the Cosway Street Evening Institute.

58 The Bermondsey Settlement LCC Inspectors Report (April 1931).

59 Ibid.

60 Keetons Road Evening Institute Log Book 1913–37.

61 Bermondsey Settlement LCC Inspector's Report (21 February 1924).

62 Keetons Road Evening Institute Log Book (January 1920).

63 Report of His Majesty's Inspectors on the Bermondsey, Rotherhithe and Fair Street Council School Evening Institute (March 1928).

64 Keetons Road Evening Institute Log Book.

65 Ibid. (January 1920).

66 Bermondsey Settlement LCC Inspectors Report (8 February 1921).

67 Bermondsey Settlement Syllabus, Lectures, Classes, Recreations (September 1921–June 1922).

68 Report on the Bermondsey Settlement (April 1931).

69 Bermondsey Settlement LCC Inspector's Report (29 March 1931).

70 Ibid. (1922).

Chapter 3

1 Montague, L. H. (1904), 'The girl in the background', in E. J. Urwick (ed.), *Studies of Boy Life in Our Cities*, London: J.M. Dent & Company, 233–54.

2 Clarke et al., *Subcultures and Cultures*, 22.

3 Soland, B. (2000), *Becoming Modern: Young Women and the Reconstruction of Womanhood in the 1920s*, Princeton, NJ: Princeton University Press, 3.

4 Ibid., 8.

5 Driscol, C. (2002), *Girls: Feminine Adolescence in Popular Cultural History*, New York: Columbia University Press, 2.

6 Hall, S. and Jefferson, T., eds (1976), *Resistance Through Rituals: Youth Subcultures in Post-War Britain,* London: Hutchinson in Association with the Centre for Contemporary Cultural Studies, University of Birmingham, 9.

7 For an appraisal of Hall's work, it is useful to look at Dyhouse, *Girls Growing Up*, who has provided an excellent critique of the impact of the notion of adolescent girlhood which evolved from the body of research and interest about the development of 'youth' from the latter part of the nineteenth century.

8 Tinkler, *Cause for Concern*, 241.

9 Gillis, *Youth and History*, 133.

10 *The Girls' Friendly Society Workers' Journal* (June 1920), 8.

11 *The Girls' Club Journal* (January 1922), 14 (40): 5.

12 *The Girls' Club Journal* (January 1925), 17 (49): 18.

13 *The Girls' Club Journal* (October 1929), 42.

14 *The Leisure of the People: A Handbook Being the Report of the National Conference held at Manchester* (November 1919), 17–20.

15 Burns, *Leisure in the Modern World*, 194.

16 Soland, *Becoming*, 7.

17 *Girls' Club Journal – Federation of Working Girls' Clubs* (February 1918), 10 (28): 6–7.

18 Ibid., 12.

19 Soland, *Becoming*.

20 *Daily Mail* (4 April 1920), 11.

21 Montague in Urwick, *Studies of Boy Life*, 233–54.

22 Beddoe, *Back to Home*, 3–4.

23 Ibid., 48.

24 *Handbook of London Trades Clothing Trades Part 1. Girls*. Advisory Committee for Juvenile Employment. Women's Library Girls Friendly Society, 7 DMB/19 Box 134.

25 Mess, H. A. (1920), *The Facts of Poverty*, London: Student Christian Movement, 115. In Durant, *The Problem of Leisure*, 87.

26 Chamberlain, M. (1989), *Growing Up In Lambeth*, London: Virago, 46.

27 Mary.

28 Maude.

29 P. P., 'Report of Women's, Advisory Committee of the Ministry of Reconstruction on the Domestic Service Problem', Cmd. 67, 1919, XX1X 8. In Lewis, J. (1984), *Women in England 1870–1950, Sexual Divisions and Social Change*, Hemel Hempstead: Harvester-Wheatsheaf, 191.

30 Letter from Miss Massey, 2 December 1916, Cosway Evening Institute.

31 Stephen, J., 'Learn to Play: Golf and Tennis for the Workers', *Bermondsey Labour Magazine* 9, 2, New Series (December 1920), 2.

32 *The Girls' Club Journal – Federation of Working Girls' Clubs* (May 1921), 12 (38): 18.

33 Giles, *Women, Identity*, 41.

34 Ibid., 36.

35 Roberts, *A Woman's Place*, 127.

36 The Pilgrim Trust (1938), *Men without Work, a Report made to the Pilgrim Trust*, Cambridge: Cambridge University Press, 230–1.

37 Lily.

38 London Advisory Council for Juvenile Employment (1928), *A Guide to Employment for London Boys and Girls*, London: HMSO, 7.

39 Report of the Bermondsey Borough Council Education Committee (5 October 1933).

40 Clara.

41 Roberts, *A Woman's Place*, 39.

42 Gamble, R. (1979), *Chelsea Child*, Bath: Chivers, 122.

43 Langhamer, *Women's Leisure*, 102–3; Davies, *Leisure, Gender*, 85–6.

44 Glucksmann, *Women Assemble*, 40; White, *Campbell Bunk*, 163.

45 Glucksmann, *Women Assemble*, 3.

46 Llewellyn Smith, *New Survey*, 5, 10.

47 Glucksmann, *Women Assemble*, 63.

48 Llewellyn Smith, *New Survey*, 2, 48.

49 Llewellyn Smith, *New Survey*, 2; London Industries I 19.

50 Ibid.

51 Beauchamp, J. (1937),*Women Who Work*, London: Laurence & Wishart, 20.

52 Priestley, *English Journey*, 129.

53 Jephcott, P. (1942), *Girls Growing Up*, London: Faber & Faber, 83.

54 Ibid.

55 Rooff, *Youth and Leisure*, 77.

56 Durant, *The Problem of Leisure*, 89–90.

57 Harley, J. L. (1937), 'Report of an enquiry into the occupations, further education and leisure interests of a number of girl wage earners from elementary and central schools in the Manchester district, with special reference to the influence of school training on their use of leisure', unpublished Med thesis, University of Manchester, 45–6. In Fowler, *The First Teenagers*, 64.

58 Jephcott, *Girls*, 86.

59 Yeo, E. M. and Yeo, S., eds (1980), *Ways of Seeing: Control and Leisure Versus Class and Struggle*, Brighton: Harvester Press, 149.

60 Holtby, W. (1934), *Women and a Changing Civilization*, London: J. Lane, The Bodley Head, 117.

61 Jephcott, *Rising Twenty*, 16.

62 Todd, S. (2005), *Young Women, Work and Family 1918–1950*, Oxford: Oxford University Press, 44–5.

63 Holtby, *Women*, 117.

64 Lil.

65 Summary of the Proceedings of a Conference on Juvenile Delinquency, London County Council (27 January 1936), 2.

66 Beauchamp, *Women who Work*, 22.

67 *Bermondsey Labour Magazine* (September 1921), 18, 2.

68 White, *The Worst Street*, 190.

69 McKibbin, R. (1998), *Classes & Cultures: England 1919–1951*, Oxford: Oxford University Press, 123.

70 Todd, *Young Women*, 114.

71 Summary of the Proceedings of a Conference on Juvenile Delinquency, London County Council (27 January 1936), 2.

72 Fowler, *The First Teenagers*, 25.

73 McKibbin, *Classes and Cultures*, 135.

74 Reid, A. (1894), *The New Party*, London: Hodder Bros, 318.

75 See, for example, Jewkes, J. and Jewkes, S. (1938), *The Juvenile Labour Market*, London: Gollancz; Cardog Jones, *The Social Survey*.

76 White, *The Worst Street*; Todd, *Young Women*, 95; McKibbin, *Classes and Cultures*, 121.

77 Alice.

78 Glucksmann, *Women Assemble*, 6.

79 'Thanks to Fashion Fad' (1929), *Western Gazette* (8 February), 2.

80 Roberts, *The Classic Slum*, 222.

81 *Girls Friendly Society Journal* (January 1920), 2.

82 Llewellyn Smith, *New Survey*, 2, 439.

83 *The Girls' Club Journal – Federation of Working Girls' Clubs* (January 1926), 18 (52): 12–14.

84 Iris.

85 *The Girls' Club Journal* (May 1921), 12 (38): 22.

86 *The Girls' Club Journal* (October 1927), 18 (57): 89–90.

Chapter 4

1 'The 1920 Girl' (1920), *The Times*, London, England (5 February), 9.

2 'Modern Women' (1921), *Yorkshire Post and Leeds Intelligencer* (29 June), 5.

3 'Girls' and Night Clubs Tales of Sordid Tragedy. Vicar's Views' (1922), *Western Daily Press* (16 May), 7.

4 'Modern Girl's Modes' (1928), *Sunday Times*, London, England (21 October), 19.

5 'The Modern Girl' (1925), *Sunday Times*, London, England (22 March), 12.

6 'Girl and Night Clubs Drunkenness in Car a Sequel to Visit' (1926), *Western Morning News* (24 April), 7.

7 'Bobbed Hair Approved' (1922), *Sunday Times*, London, England (12 March), 13.

8 'She Prefers Viking Chocolates' (1925), *Illustrated London News*, London, England (14 February), 1.

9 'Age Views Youth Dame Ethel Smythe and the Modern Girl' (1928), *Western Daily Press* (24 April), 12.

10 'Bitter Attack on Modern Girls' (1924), *Evening Telegraph* (19 March), 3.

11 Llewellyn Smith, *New Survey*, 9, 47.

12 Hall, S. (1977), 'Culture, the media and the ideology effect', in Curran, J., Gurevitch, M. and Wollacott, J. (eds), *Mass Communication and Society*, London: Edward Arnold Publishers Ltd, in association with the Open University Press, 315–48.

13 Llewellyn Smith, *New Survey*, 9, 45.

14 Ibid., 45–6.

15 Ibid., 43.

16 Rowson, S., 'A statistical survey of the cinema industry in Great Britain in 1934', in *Journal of the Royal Statistical Society*, in Richards, J. (1984), *The Age of the Dream Palace: Cinema and Society in Britain 1930–1939*, London: Routledge & Kegan Paul, 13.

17 Carr, R. 'World Film News' 1, no. 10, January 1937, in Richards, *The Age of the Dream*, 13.

18 'News in Brief' (1920), *The Times*, London, England (14 June), 12.

19 *The Bermondsey Book: A Quarterly Review of Life and Literature* (September 1926), London: Cecil Palmer, 3 (4): 95.

20 Report of a Meeting for Branch Presidents, Secretaries and All Workers (18 May 1936), in *The Girls' Friendly Society Review* (1935), 69, 124–5. Minutes of *The Girls' Friendly Society* (August 1936).

21 Bakke, E. W. (1938), *The Unemployed Man: A Social Study*, London: Nisbet, 181.

22 For example, Jephcott, *Girls*, 116.

23 Fowler, *The First Teenagers*, 113.

24 Enstad, *Ladies of Labor*, 162.

25 Rooff, *Youth and Leisure*, 85.

26 Lil.

27 Spring Rice, *Working-Class Wives*, 109–15.

28 *The Bermondsey Book*, 98.

29 'Positively Immoral' (1927), *Western Daily Press* (20 August), 7.

30 Buckman, P. (1978), *Let's Dance: Social, Ballroom and Folk Dancing*, London: Paddington Press, 156.

31 'The Mania of the Moment Dancing' (1919), *The Daily Mail* (8 January), 7.

32 Samuel, R. and Light, A. (1994) 'Doing the Lambeth Walk', in *Theatres of Memory*, London: Verso, 1, 390–400.

33 Rust, F. (1969), *Dance in Society: An Analysis of the Relationship Between the Social Dance and Society in England From the Middle Ages to the Present Day*, London: Routledge & Kegan Paul, 86.

34 Jephcott, *Girls*, 115.

35 Over the water was a reference to the opposite bank of the river Thames.

36 Jessie.

37 Llewellyn Smith, *New Survey*, 9, 47.

38 *Girls' Friendly Society Review* (August 1936), 125.

39 White, C. L. (1970), *Women's Magazines 1690–1968*, London: M. Joseph, 95.

40 Ibid., 97.

41 Tinkler, *Constructing Girlhood*, 45.

42 White, *Women's Magazines*, 98.

43 Tinkler, *Constructing Girlhood*, 57.

44 Clara.

45 Beddoe, *Back to Home*, 8.

46 Tinkler, *Women's Magazines*, 4.

47 Durant, *The Problem of Leisure*, 93.

48 Tinkler, *Constructing Girlhood*, 184.

49 Holtby, *Women*, 118.

50 Ibid., 19.

51 Soland, *Becoming Modern*, 4.

52 'The Woman of To-day (1920)', *The Times* (20 January), 13.

53 Soland, *Becoming Modern*, 21.

54 Lewis, *Women in England*, 4–7; Beddoe, *Back to Home*, 3.

55 Priestley, *English Journey*, 95.

56 *The Biscuit Box*, Journal of the Employees of Peek Frean and Co Ltd (February 1922), 58.

57 Ibid. (October 1923), 178.

58 Ibid. (August 1920), 2 (10): 151.

59 *Bermondsey Labour Magazine* (June 1921), 15, 12.

60 Ibid. (September 1925), 21, 4.

61 Ibid. (March 1924), 6, 5.

62 Ibid. (June 1931), 5.

63 Ibid. (May 1927), 40, 7–8.

64 Ibid. (July 1927) 42, 3.

65 Jessie; Lil; Ivy.

66 'Councils Edict on Female Football' (1921), *Western Gazette* (9 December), 3.

67 'Girl Wrestlers Form a Club' (1928), *Evening Telegraph* (3 February), 7.

68 *The Girls' Friendly Society* (February 1928), 3.

69 *The Girls' Club Journal* (January 1925), 17 (49): 11.

70 Willis, P. (1977), *Learning to Labour: How Working-Class Kids get Working-Class Jobs*, Farnborough: Saxon House, 36.

71 *The Girls' Friendly Society Workers' Journal* (January 1933), 626 New Series 7.

72 Ibid.

73 The Cosway Street Women's Institute Log Book (1916).

74 *The Workers' Journal Girls' Friendly Society* (January 1934), 11.

75 Ibid., 34.

76 *The Girls' Club Journal* (January 1934), 25 (76): 1.

77 *Girls' Club Journal, Federation of Working Girls' Clubs* (January 1920), 16 (64): 11.

78 *The Girls' Friendly Society Journal* (March 1934), 34.

79 *The Girls' Club Journal* (January 1928), 9 (58): 3.

80 *The Girls' Friendly Society* (6 July 1938), 136–7.

81 *The Girls' Club Journal* (January 1922), 14 (40): 4.

82 Llewellyn Smith, *London Life*, 9, 5.

83 Clara.

84 Lil.

85 Ibid.

86 See Davies, *Leisure, Gender*.

87 Llewellyn Smith, *New Survey*, respondent vi, 9, 246.

88 Llewellyn Smith, *New Survey*, respondent ii, 9, 246.

89 *Girls' Friendly Society*, Report of the Committee for Extension Work, 3 March 1922.

90 Llewellyn Smith, *New Survey*, respondent iii, 9, 246.

91 O'Neill, G. (1990), *Pull No More Bines Hop Picking: Memories of a Vanished Way of Life*, London: The Women's Press, 54–5.

Chapter 5

1 'The most optimistic place in London. Introducing Bermondsey, with its flowers and pretty girls', *Evening Standard* (1930), 29 September: 19.

2 See, for example, Jones, *Workers at Play*; Fowler, *The First Teenagers*; Osgerby, *Youth in Britain*; Davies, *Leisure, Gender*.

3 Durant, *The Problem*, 77.

4 Abrams, *The First Teenagers*, 10.

5 Fowler, *The First Teenagers*, 110.

6 Durant, *The Problem*, 78.

7 Harley, *Report*, 157. In Fowler, *The First Teenagers*, 110.

8 Langhamer, *Women's Leisure*, 2.

9 Enstad, *Ladies of Labor*, 50.

10 Clarke, J., Hall, S., Jefferson, T. and Roberts, B. (1975), 'Subcultures, cultures and class', in Hall, S. and Jefferson, T., eds, *Resistance Through Rituals: Youth Subcultures in Post-War Britain*, London: Hutchinson, for The Centre for Contemporary Cultural Studies, University of Birmingham, 44.

11 Clarke and Critcher, *The Devil*, 50.

12 Roberts, *A Woman's Place*, 42–3.

13 Kathy.

14 Ivy.

15 Jessie.

16 Kathy.

17 Sarah.

18 Lizzie.

19 Kathy.

20 Kathy.

21 Sarah.

22 Iris.

23 Mary McQillan in Fagan S. (1997), *Born in Bermondsey*, London: (s.l.), 39.

24 Walton and Walvin, *Leisure in Britain*, 134.

25 Bakke, *The Unemployed*, 182.

26 *Bermondsey Labour Magazine* (December 1920), 9 (2 New Series), 2.

27 Mitchell, S. (1995), *The New Girl: Girls' Culture in England 1880–1915*, New York: Columbia University Press, 4.

28 Alexander, *Becoming*, 205.

29 Melman, B. (1988), *Women and the Popular Imagination in the Twenties: Flappers and Nymphs*, London: Macmillan, 8.

30 Hoggart, R. (1963), *The Uses of Literacy*, London: Penguin, 51.

31 Roberts, *A Woman's Place*, 11.

32 Jessie.

33 Richards, J. (1984), *The Age of the Dream Palace: Cinema and Society in Britain 1930–1939*, London: Routledge & Kegan Paul, 156.

34 Kathy.

35 Llewellyn Smith, *New Survey*, 9, 47.

36 *Bermondsey Labour Magazine* (July 1927), 42, 8.

37 Ibid. (October 1934), 121, 4.

38 *Girls' Friendly Society Journal* (May 1936), 77.

39 McKibbin, *Classes and Cultures*, 390.

40 Kathy.

41 Maude.

42 *Bermondsey Labour Magazine* (December 1928), 57, 5.

43 *Bermondsey Labour Magazine* (December 1926), 35, 15.

44 Lucy.

45 Jessie.

46 Mowat, C. (1955), *Britain Between the Wars: 1918–1940*, London: Methuen, 213.

47 Meacham, S. (1977), *A Life Apart: The English Working-Class 1890–1914*, London: Thames and Hudson, 26.

48 Johnson, R. (1979), 'Culture and historians', in Clarke, J., Critcher, C. and Johnson, R., eds, *Working Class Culture: Studies in Theory and History*, London: Hutchinson Press, in Association with the Centre for Contemporary Cultural Studies, University of Birmingham, 62.

49 Booth, C. (1902), *The Life and Labour of the People of London*, London: Macmillan, 1, 130–1.

50 Cambridge University Mission Minutes of Committee Meeting 1920.

51 Jessie.

52 Harris, C. (1927), *The Uses of Leisure in Bethnal Green: A Survey of Social Conditions in the Borough 1925–1926*, London: Lindsay Press, 51–2.

53 Alice.

54 Inspector's Report Bermondsey Settlement (24 March 1931).

55 Report of His Majesty's Inspectors on The Bermondsey, Rotherhithe, Fair Street Council School Evening Institute 1928.

56 Lucy.

57 The tick book was the book in which account was kept of how much credit an individual had and how much he or she had repaid.

58 Eileen Margaret Cassey in Fagan, *Born in Bermondsey*, London: (s.l.), 182.

59 Roberts, *The Classic Slum*, 82.

60 Lucy.

61 Hoggart, *The Uses*, 61.

62 Emmy.

63 Margaret.

64 Clara.

65 Kathy.

66 Alice.

67 Peiss, *Cheap Amusements*, 63.

68 White, *The Worst Street*, 192.

69 Paterson, A. (1912), *Across the Bridges*, London: Arnold, 37.

70 Enstad, *Ladies of Labor*, 2.

71 Fyvel, T. R. (1961), *The Insecure Offenders: Rebellious Youth in the Welfare State*, London: Chatto &. Windus, 48.

72 Holtby, *Women*, 118.

73 Cohen, P. (1972), *Subcultural, Conflict & Working Class Communities*, Working Papers in Cultural Studies No. 2, Centre for Contemporary Cultural Studies, University of Birmingham.

74 Kathy.

75 Tebbutt, *Women's Talk*, 149.

76 Chamberlain, *Growing Up*, 67.

77 Ibid.

78 'Too Much Lipstick (1927)', *Gloucestershire Echo* (8 August): 5.

79 *Gloucester Citizen* (8 April 1932): 8.

80 'Bank Girls Make-up Dark Dresses and No Paint' (1932), *Gloucester Citizen*, (8 April): 8.

81 *The Girls' Friendly Society Workers' Journal* (March 1935), 20.

82 *The City Press* (28 April 1928).

83 Chamberlain, *Growing Up*, 68.

84 Kathy.

85 Annie Howell in Fagan, *Born in Bermondsey*, 12.

86 Peiss, *Cheap Amusements*, 57.

87 Enstad, *Ladies of Labor*, 6.

88 Ibid., 68.

Chapter 6

1 Priestley, *English Journey*, 402–3.

2 Lil.

3 Burke, T. (1934), *London in My Time*, London: Rich and Cowan, 65–6.

4 See Tinkler, *Cause for Concern*, for an excellent overview of how the girl became the subject of scrutiny.

5 Hall, S. and Jefferson, T., eds (1976), *Resistance Through Rituals: Subcultures in Post-War Britain*, London: Hutchinson, 9.

6 Giles, J. (1992), '"Playing hard to get": Working-class women, sexuality and respectability in Britain, 1918–1940', *Women's History Review* 1 (2): 239–55, 242.

7 Booth, C. (1889), *London Life and Labour*, London: Williams and Norgate, 147.

8 Chinn, C. (1991), *Better Betting with a Decent Fella*, London: Harvester Wheatsheaf, 59.

9 Tebbutt, *Women's Talk?* 142.

10 Booth, C. (1903), *Life and Labour of the People in London*, London: Macmillan, 2, 127.

11 Llewellyn Smith, *The New Survey*, 3, 357.

12 Roberts, *The Classic Slum*, 17.

13 See, for example, the archives of The Girls' Friendly Society and The National Organisation of Girls' Clubs for an overview of these debates.

14 Meacham, S. (1977), *A Life Apart: The English Working-Class 1890–1914*, London: Thames & Hudson, 118.

15 Iris Danne in Fagan, S. (1997), *Born in Bermondsey*, London: (s.l.).

16 Jessie.

17 See, for example, Roberts, *A Woman's Place*; Hoggart, *The Uses of Literacy*; Roberts, *The Classic Slum*; Peiss, *Cheap Amusements*; Chinn, *Better Betting*.

18 Margaret.

19 White, *The Worst Street*, 57.

20 Bakke, *The Unemployed*, 182.

21 Mary.

22 Lil.

23 Tebbutt, *Women's Talk*, 149.

24 Ibid., 143.

25 See, for example, Hoggart, *The Uses*; Roberts, *The Classic Slum*; Davies, *Leisure, Gender*.

26 White, *The Worst Street*, 6.

27 Peiss, *Cheap Amusements*, 57.

28 Enstad, *Ladies of Labor*, 13.

29 For an excellent discussion about the concept of community, see Roberts, *A Woman's Place*; Chamberlain, *Growing Up*; Bourke, *Working-Class*, Chap. 5.

30 See, for example, Gamble, *Chelsea Child*; Bennett, H. J. (1980), *I was a Walworth Boy*, Peckham: Peckham Publishing Project; Foakes, G. (1974), *Between High Walls: A London Childhood*, Oxford: Athena Books.

31 'Youth and Leisure New Generation that Lacks Sense of Responsibility. Maintaining Present Standards' (1935), *The Manchester Guardian* (20 February), 2.

32 Rooff, *Youth and Leisure*, 3.

33 Ibid., 184.

34 Humphries, *Hooligans*, 5.

35 *The Girls' Friendly Society Journal* (January 1924), 7.

36 Harris, *The Uses of Leisure in Bethnal Green*, 51–2.

37 Address given by Mr Kennedy Cox of the Docklands Settlement at the Annual Council and Conference of the Executive Committee and Club Leaders in *The Girls' Club Journal* (January 1922), 14 (40): 4.

38 Paterson, *Across the Bridges*, 141–4.

39 Durant, *The Problem*, 89.

40 Cosway Street Women's Institute Log Book 1919.

41 *Girls' Friendly Society Workers Journal* (November 1928).

42 *The Girls' Club Journal* (October 1921), 12, 39, 43.

43 Dewar, K. (1921), *The Girl*, London: G. Bell & Sons Ltd, 9.

44 Peiss, *Cheap Amusements*, 14.

45 Mary.

46 Gladys Shrewsbury, in Fagan, *Born in Bermondsey*, 100.

47 Lil.

48 Richards, *The Age of the Dream Palace*, 169.

49 Peiss, *Cheap Amusements*, 33.

50 Richards, *The Age of the Dream Palace*, 70.

51 Cited in Machin, G. I. T. (1989), *Churches and Social Issues in Twentieth Century Britain*, Oxford: Claredon Press, 79.

52 *Girls' Friendly Society Magazine* (January 1923).

53 *The Girls' Club Journal* (May 1921), 21, 38, 19.

54 *Girls' Friendly Society Workers Journal* (January 1933), 7.

55 *Girls' Friendly Society Review* (April 1933), 56–7.

56 *Girls' Friendly Society Review* (October 1935).

57 *The Girls' Club Journal* (February 1917), 9 (25): 8–9.

58 *Girls' Friendly Society Magazine* (January 1923), 19.

59 Girls' Friendly Society Central Council 25/10/1927 Agenda Book.

60 'East End Changes. What Mr. Charrington has Seen in Fifty Years: Evils of the Cinema' (1920), *Observer* (8 February): 8.

61 *Cherio!* (November 1934), St James Church Parish Magazine, 1, no. 11.

62 Girls' Friendly Society, Minutes of the Central Council (15 March 1938).

63 Humphries, *Hooligans*, 130.

64 Emmy.

65 Chinn, *Better Betting*, 59.

66 Giles, *Playing Hard to Get*, 243.

67 Clara.

68 Emmy.

69 Lil.

70 Margaret.

71 Kathy.

72 Margaret.

73 Green et al., *Women's Leisure, What Leisure?*, 47.

74 Air raid protection.

75 Lil.

76 Mr Kennedy Cox, Address (4 January 1922), 14 (40): 4.

77 Llewellyn Smith, *The New Survey*, 9, 258.

78 'The Cocktail Habit. Bishop of London's Warning to Young Girls' (1926), *The Sunday Times*, (28 February): 20.

79 'Advised to Shun All Betting and Cocktails' (1933), *Nottingham Evening Post* (16 February): 3.

80 Tinkler, P. (2001), 'Red tips for hot lips: Advertising cigarettes for young women in Britain, 1920–1970', *Women's History Review*, 10 (2): 249–72, 253.

81 *The Biscuit Box* (1919), 4, 59.

82 Lil.

83 Alice.

84 Giles, *Playing Hard to Get*, 243.

85 Orwell, G. in Richards, *The Age of the Dream Palace*, 159.

86 Jessie.

87 Jessie.

88 Lebas, E. (1995), 'When every street became a cinema: The film work of Bermondsey Borough Council's Public Health Department 1923–1953', *History Workshop Journal*, 39 (1): 43–66.

89 Wearing, B. M. (1992), 'Leisure and women's identity in late adolescence', *Society and Leisure*, 15: 325–45.

90 See, for example, Shaw, S. M. (2001), 'Conceptualizing resistance: Women's leisure as political practice', *Journal of Leisure Research*, 33 (2): 186–201. Also Green et al., *Women's Leisure.*

91 Wearing, B. M. (1990), 'Leisure and Women's Identity'. Paper presented at the XIIth Congress of the International Sociological Association, Madrid: Spain, 9–13 July. In Wearing, B., Wearing, S. and Kelly. K., 'Adolescent women, identity and smoking: Leisure experience as resistance', *Sociology of Health and Illness*, 16 (5): 623–26, 628.

92 Enstad, *Ladies of Labor*, 6.

93 Jackson, C. and Tinkler, P. (2007), '"Laddettes" and "modern girls": "Troublesome" young femininities', *The Sociological Review*, 55 (2): 251–72, 254. Also see the work of Dyhouse, *Girls Growing Up.*

94 White, *The Worst Street*, 190.

95 Ibid., 191.

96 'Photo Report, Manicure for Girls' (1928), *Daily Herald* (23 August): 6.

97 Tebbutt, *Women's Talk*, 149.

98 Davies, *Leisure, Gender*, 111.

99 Humphries, *Hooligans*, 122.

100 Ibid.

101 Martin, A. (July 1911), *The Married Working Woman*, London: National Union of Suffrage Societies, 11.

102 McRobbie, A. (1991), *Feminism and Youth Culture: From Jackie to Just Seventeen*, Boston: Unwin Hyman, 13.

103 Green, E. (1998), '"Women doing friendship": An analysis of women's leisure as a site of identity construction, empowerment and resistance', *Leisure Studies*, 17 (3): 171–85.

Afterword

1 Alice.

2 Glucksmann, *Women Assemble.*

Select bibliography

Books and chapters

Abrams, L. (2010), *Oral History Theory*, Oxford: Routledge.

Abrams, M. (1950), *The Teenage Consumer: Teenage Consumer Spending in 1959*. Part 11, London: Press Exchange.

Alexander, S. (1994), 'Becoming a Woman in London in the 1920s and '30s', in S. Alexander (ed.), *Becoming a Woman and Other Essays in 19th and 20th Century Feminist History*, 203–24, London: Virago.

Bakke, E. W. (1933), *The Unemployed Man: A Social Study*, London: Nisbet & Co.

Beauchamp, J. (1937), *Women Who Work*, London: Lawrence and Wishart.

Beddoe, D. (1989), *Back to Home and Duty: Women Between the Wars 1918–1939*, London: Pandora.

Bennett, H. J. (1980), *I was a Walworth Boy*, Peckham: Peckham Publishing Project.

Beveridge, W. H. (1930), *Unemployment: A Problem of Industry*, 2nd edn, London: Longmans.

Booth, C. (1889), *London Life and Labour of the People of London. 1*, London: Williams and Norgate.

Booth, C. (1903), *Life and Labour of the People in London, 2*, London: Macmillan.

Borland, K. (1991), '"That's not what I said": Interpretative Conflict in Oral Narrative Research', in S. B. Gluck and D. Patai (eds), *Women's Words: The Feminist Practice of Oral History*, 63–75, London: Routledge.

Bourke, J. (1994), *Working-Class Cultures in Britain 1890–1960*, London: Routledge.

Buckman, P. (1978), *Let's Dance: Social, Ballroom and Folk Dancing*, London: Paddington Press.

Burke, T. (1934), *London in My Time*, London: Rich and Cowan.

Burns, C. D. (1932), *Leisure in the Modern World*, London: Allen & Unwin.

Cardog Jones, D. (1934), *The Social Survey of Merseyside*, Liverpool: Liverpool University Press.

Chamberlain, M. (1989), *Growing Up in Lambeth*, London: Virago.

Chinn, C. (1991), *Better Betting with a Decent Fella*, London: Harvester Wheatsheaf.

Clarke, C. and Critcher, C. (1979), *Working-Class Culture: Studies in History and Theory*, London: Hutchinson.

Clarke, J. and Critcher, C. (1985), *The Devil Makes Work: Leisure in Capitalist Britain*, Basingstoke: Macmillan.

Cohen, P. (1972), *Subcultural, Conflict & Working Class Communities*, Working Papers in Cultural Studies No. 2, Centre for Contemporary Cultural Studies, University of Birmingham.

Curran, J., Gurevitch, M. and Wollacott, J., eds (1979), *Mass Communication and Society*, London: Edward Arnold.

Cutten, G. B. (1926), *The Threat of Leisure*, New Haven: Yale University Press.

Davis, J. (1990), *Youth and the Condition of Britain: Images of Adolescent Conflict*, London: Athlone.

Davies, A. (1992), *Leisure, Gender and Poverty: Working-Class Culture in Salford and Manchester 1900–1939*, Buckingham: Open University Press.

Deem, R. (1986), *All Work and No Play? The Sociology of Leisure*, Milton Keynes: Open University Press.

Delise Burns, C. (1932), *Leisure in the Modern World*, London: Allen & Unwin.

Devereux, W. A. (1982), *Adult Education in Inner London 1870–1980*, London: Shepheard-Walwyn.

Dewar, K. (1921), *The Girl*, London: G. Bell & Sons Ltd.

Driscol, C. (2002), *Girls: Feminine Adolescence in Popular Cultural History*, New York: Columbia University Press.

Durant, H. (1938), *The Problem of Leisure*, London: Routledge and Sons.

Dyhouse, C. (1981), *Girls Growing Up in Late Victorian and Edwardian England*, London: Routledge and Kegan Paul.

Enstad, N. (1999), *Ladies of Labor, Girls of Adventure: Working Women, Popular Culture, and Labor Politics at the Turn of the Twentieth Century*, New York. Columbia University Press.

Foakes, G. (1974), *Between High Walls: A London Childhood*, Oxford: Athena Books.

Fowler, D. (1995), *The First Teenagers: The Lifestyles of Young Wage-Earners in Interwar Britain*, London: Woburn Press.

Fyvel, T. R. (1961), *The Insecure Offenders: Rebellious Youth in the Welfare State*, London: Chatto and Windus.

Gamble, R. (1979), *Chelsea Child*, Bath: Chivers.

Giles, J. (1995), *Women, Identity and Private Life in Britain, 1900–50*, Basingstoke: Macmillan.

Gillis, J. (1974), *Youth and History: Tradition and Change in European Age Relations 1770–Present*, New York & London: Academic Press.

Glucksmann, M. (1990), *Women Assemble: Women Workers in the New Industries of Interwar Britain*, London: Routledge.

Green, E., Hebron, S. and Woodward, D. (1990), *Women's Leisure. What Leisure?* Basingstoke: Macmillan.

Greenwood, W. (1933), *Love on the Dole*, London: Penguin.

Hall, S. and Jefferson, T., eds (1976), *Resistance Through Rituals: Youth Subcultures in Post-War Britain*, London: Hutchinson in Association with the Centre for Contemporary Cultural Studies, University of Birmingham.

Harris, C. (1927), *The Uses of Leisure in Bethnal Green: A Survey of Social Conditions in the Borough 1925–1926*, London: Lindsay Press.

Hendrick, H. (1990), *Images of Youth: Age, Class and the Male Youth Problem, 1880–1920*, Oxford: Clarendon Press.

Hoggart, R. (1963), *The Uses of Literacy*, London: Penguin.

Holtby, W. (1936), *Women and a Changing Civilisation*, London: John Lane The Bodley Head.

Howkins, A. and Lowerson, J. (1979), *Trends in Leisure 1919–1939, A Review for the Joint Panel on Leisure & Recreation Research*, London: The Sports Council and Social Science Research Council.

Humphries, S. (1981), *Hooligans or Rebels? An Oral History of Working-Class Childhood and Youth, 1889–1939*, Oxford: Basil Blackwell.

Hutt, A. (1933), *The Condition of the Working-Class in Britain*, London: M. Lawrence Ltd.

Jephcott, A. P. (1942), *Girls Growing Up*, London: Faber & Faber.

Jewkes, J. and Jewkes, S. (1938), *The Juvenile Labour Market*, London: Gollancz.

Jones, D. C., ed. (1934), *The Social Survey of Merseyside*, Liverpool: Liverpool University Press.

Jones, S. G. (1986), *Workers at Play: A Social and Economic History of Leisure*, London: Routledge and Kegan Paul.

Langhamer, C. (2000), *Women's Leisure in England 1920–1960*, Manchester: Manchester University Press.

Leff, V. and Blunden, C. H. (1900–65), *Riverside Story: The Story of Bermondsey and its People*, produced and published by Civic Publicity Services Ltd.

Lewis, J. (1984), *Women in England 1870–1950, Sexual Divisions and Social Change*, Hemel Hempstead: Harvester-Wheatsheaf.

Lindsay, K. (1926), *Social Progress and Educational Waste: Being a Study of the 'Free-Place' and Scholarship System etc*, London: G. Routledge and Sons.

Llewellyn Smith, H., ed. (1935), *The New Survey of London Life and Labour*, London: P.S. King.

Martin, A. (1911), *The Married Working Woman*, London: National Union of Suffrage Societies.

McKibbin, R. (1998), *Classes and Cultures: England 1918–1951*, Oxford: Oxford University Press.

McRobbie, A. (1991), *Feminism and Youth Culture: From Jackie to Just Seventeen*, Boston: Unwin Hyman.

Meacham, S. (1997), *A Life Apart: The English Working-Class 1890–1914*, London: Thames and Hudson.

Melman, B. (1988), *Women and the Popular Imagination in the Twenties: Flappers and Nymphs*, London: Macmillan.

Mitchell, S. (1995), *The New Girl: Girls' Culture in England 1880–1915*, New York: Columbia University Press.

Montague, L. H. (1904), 'The Girl in the Background', in E. J. Urwick (ed.), *Studies of Boy Life in our Cities*, 233–54, London: J.M. Dent & Company.

Mowatt, C. (1955), *Britain Between the Wars: 1918–1940*, London: Methuen.

O'Neill, G. (1990), *Pull No More Bines Hop Picking: Memories of a Vanished Way of Life*, London: The Women's Press.

Orwell, G. (1937), *The Road to Wigan Pier*, London: Victor Gollancz.

Osgerby, B. (1998), *Youth in Britain Since 1945*, Oxford: Blackwell.

Parratt, C. M. (2001), *'More Than Mere Amusement' Working-Class Women's Leisure in England. 1750–1914*, Boston: Northeastern University Press.

Paterson, A. (1911), *Across the Bridges*, London: Edward Arnold.

Peiss, K. (1986), *Cheap Amusements: Working Women and Leisure in Turn of the Century New York*, Philadelphia: Temple University Press.

Priestley, J. B. (1940), *English Journey*, London: William Heinemann Ltd and Victor Gollancz Ltd.

Reid, A. (1984), *The New Party*, London: Hodder.

Richards, J. (1984), *The Age of the Dream Palace: Cinema and Society in Britain. 1930–1939*, London: Routledge and Kegan Paul.

Roberts, E. (1985), *A Woman's Place: An Oral History of Working-Class Women 1890–1940*, Oxford: Blackwell.

Roberts, R. (1973), *The Classic Slum: Salford Life in the First Quarter of the Century*, Middlesex: Pelican.

Rooff, M. (1935), *Youth and Leisure*, Edinburgh: T & A Constable.

Rowntree, S. B. (1941), *Poverty and Progress: A Second Social Survey of York*, London: Longmans.

Rust, F. (1969), *Dance in Society: An Analysis of the Relationship Between the Social Dance and Society in England From the Middle Ages to the Present Day*, London: Routledge and Kegan Paul.

Samuel, R. (1994), *Theatres of Memory, Past and Present in Contemporary Culture Part 1*, London: Verso.

Soland, B. (2000), *Becoming Modern: Young Women and the Reconstruction of Womanhood in the 1920s*, Princeton: Princeton University Press.

Spring Rice, M. (1939), *Working-Class Wives: Their Health and Conditions*, Middlesex: Pelican.

Springhall, J. (1986), *Coming of Age: Adolescence in Britain 1860-1960*, Dublin: Gill and Macmillan.

Stevenson, J. (1984), *British Society 1914–1945*, Middlesex: Allen Lane.

Tebbutt, M. (1995), *Women's Talk? A Social History of Gossip in Working-Class Neighbourhoods 1880–1960*, Aldershot: Scolar Press, 1995.

Tebbutt, M. (2012), *Being Boys: Youth, Leisure and Identity in the Inter-War Years*, Manchester: Manchester University Press.

The Pilgrim Trust (1938), *Men without Work, a Report Made to the Pilgrim Trust*, Cambridge: Cambridge University Press.

Tinkler, P. (1995), *Constructing Girlhood: Popular Magazines for Girls Growing Up in England 1920–1950*, London: Taylor and Francis.

Todd, S. (2005), *Young Women, Work and Family 1918–1950*, Oxford: University Press.

Tout, H. (1938), *The Standard of Living in Bristol*, Bristol: Arrowsmith.

Urwick, E. J., ed. (1904), *Studies of Boy Life in Our Cities*, London: J.M. Dent.

Walton, J. K. and Walvin, J., eds (1983), *Leisure in Britain 1780–1939*, Manchester: Manchester University Press.

White, C. L. (1970), *Women's Magazines 1690–1968*, London: Michael Joseph.

White, J. (1986), *The Worst Street in North London: Campbell Bunk, Islington Between the Wars*, London: Boston and Henley.

Wilkinson, E. (1939), *The Town that was Murdered: The Life-Story of Jarrow*, London: Victor Gollancz.

Willis, P. (1977), *Learning to Labour: How Working-Class Kids get Working-Class Jobs*, Farnborough: Saxon House.

Yeo, E. M. and Yeo, S., eds (1980), *Ways of Seeing: Control and Leisure Versus Class and Struggle*, Brighton: Harvester Press.

Journals and magazines

The Bermondsey Book: A Quarterly Review of Life and Literature (September 1926), London: Cecil Palmer.

Bermondsey Labour Magazine.

The Biscuit Box, the journal of the employees of Peek Freans and Co Ltd.
Cherio! St James Church Parish Magazine.
The Girls' Club Journal MS227/5/8/2/3 volumes 2 and 3.
The Girls' Friendly Society Journal 5GFS/o1/017.

Articles

Bailey, P. (1999), 'The Politics and Poetics of Modern British Leisure: A Late Twentieth Century Review', *Rethinking History*, 3 (2): 131–75.

Giles, J. (1992), '"Playing Hard to Get": Working-Class Women, Sexuality and Respectability in Britain, 1918–1940', *Women's History Review*, 1 (2): 239–55.

Green, E. (1998), '"Women Doing Friendship": An Analysis of Women's Leisure as a Site of Identity Construction, Empowerment and Resistance', *Leisure Studies*, 17 (3): 171–85.

Jackson, C. and Tinkler, P. (2007), '"Laddettes" and "Modern Girls": "Troublesome" Young Femininities', *The Sociological Review*, 55 (2 05): 251–72.

Lebas, E. (1995), 'When Every Street Became a Cinema: The Film Work of Bermondsey Borough Council's Public Health Department 1923–1953', *History Workshop Journal*, 39 (1): 43–66.

Shaw, S. M. (2001), 'Conceptualizing Resistance: Women's Leisure as Political Practice', *Journal of Leisure Research*, 33 (2): 186–201.

Tinkler, P. (2001), 'Red Tips for Hot Lips: Advertising Cigarettes for Young Women in Britain, 1920–1970', *Women's History Review*, 2 (10): 249–72.

Tinkler, P. (2003), 'Cause for Concern: Young Women and Leisure, 1930–1950', *Women's History Review*, 12 (2): 233–62.

Wearing, B. M. (1990), 'Leisure and Women's Identity'. Paper presented at the XIIth Congress of the International Sociological Association, Madrid, Spain, 9–13 July. Cited in Wearing, B., Wearing, S. and Kelly, K. (1990), 'Adolescent Women, Identity and Smoking: Leisure Experience as Resistance', *Sociology of Health and Illness*, 16 (5): 626–23.

Wearing, B. M. (1992), 'Leisure and Women's Identity in Late Adolescence', *Society and Leisure*, 15 (1992): 325–45.

Newspapers

Christchurch Messenger
City Press
Daily
Daily Herald
Evening Telegraph
Guardian
Gloucester Citizen
Gloucestershire Echo

Illustrated London News
London Evening Standard
Manchester Guardian
Observer
The Sunday Times
The Times
Western Daily Press
Western Gazette
Western Morning News
Yorkshire Post
Yorkshire Post and Leeds Intelligencer

Archives

Cambridge University Mission

Address given by Reverend E. A. B. Royds MA at the Annual General Meeting of
    the Cambridge University Mission (15 April 1926).
Cambridge University Mission Minutes of Committee Meeting 1920.
Minutes of the Cambridge University Mission (1 May 1931).
Rules and Regulations of the Mission, Cambridge University Mission Committee
    Meeting, (10 February 1922).

Southwark Local Studies Library

Bermondsey Settlement Annual Report (1892–1901).
Bermondsey Settlement Syllabus, Lectures, Classes, Recreations (September
    1921–June 1922).
Borough Polytechnic Trade School for Girls Curriculum (10 April 1934).
Report of the Bermondsey Borough Council Education Committee (5 October 1933).
Work of Men's Institutes in London (1926), The Board of Education, Pamphlet No.
    48, London: HMSO.

London Metropolitan Archives

Bermondsey Settlement LCC Inspector's Report (8 February 1921), LCC/ED/
    HFE/15/12.
Bermondsey Settlement LCC Inspector's Report (29 March 1931), LCC/ED/
    HFE/15/12.
The Bermondsey Settlement LCC Inspector's Report (April 1931), LCC/ED/
    HFE/15/12.
The Cosway Street Women's Institute Logbook (1916) LCC/EO/HFE/10/016.
Council School Evening Institute (March 1928), LCC/ED/HFE/15/12.

Keetons Road Evening Institute Logbook 1913–1937. LCC/EO/HFE/10/021.
Logbook of the Cosway Street Evening Institute LCC/EO/HFE/10/17.
London Advisory Council for Juvenile Employment (1928), *A Guide to Employment for London Boys and Girls*, London: HMSO.
Report of His Majesty's Inspectors on the Bermondsey, Rotherhithe and Fair Street.
Summary of the Proceedings of a Conference on Juvenile Delinquency, London County Council, 27 January 1936, 2. LCC/CH/D/4/6.
The Women's Library @LSE 7 DMB/23 Box file FL 134.

Theses

Abenstern, M. (1986), 'Expression and Control: A Case Study of Working-Class Leisure and Gender 1918–1939, A Case Study of Rochdale Using Oral Evidence', PhD, Essex University.
Langhamer, C. (1996), 'Women and Leisure in Manchester, 1920–c. 1960', PhD, University of Central Lancashire.

Index